PSYCHOLOGY
ENCOUNTERS JUDAISM

PSYCHOLOGY
ENCOUNTERS
JUDAISM

Joel Klein

Institute of Child Study
University of Toronto

PHILOSOPHICAL LIBRARY
NEW YORK

Copyright, 1979, by Philosophical Library, Inc.
15 East 40 Street, New York, New York 10016
All rights reserved
Library of Congress Catalog Card No. 79-84852
SBN 8022-2350-8
Manufactured in the United States of America

TO SHIFRA
MY WOMAN OF VALOR
AND TO MY PARENTS

TABLE OF CONTENTS

PREFACE

Throughout this book the word Torah sometimes refers to the Pentateuch, but more often is used as a general term to include the cumulative body of Jewish teachings.

The book is a series of essays which are connected by some central themes which reappear in different forms. Perhaps the most important theme is the conflicting ways in which one question has been answered: What is man? The level of writing presupposes little understanding of psychology and less knowledge of the Torah, the literary style having been constructed to accommodate both the curiosity of the beginner and the critical gaze of the advanced student.

The title of the book may mislead one into believing that the similarities and differences of psychology and the Torah are singular and easy to formulate. In fact, the Torah often has two or three views on a given topic, while psychology may have a dozen. This forces one to make generalizations that either oversimplify the problem or contain important exceptions whose ramifications are too elaborate to be included in the flow of the argument. Since it is impossible to say what is *the* Torah viewpoint on many issues, I have tried in each instance to allow my understanding of the Torah to guide me into formulating its major thrust. I have had little help from my predecessors in this relatively unexplored area because I concluded that they have erred, for whatever reasons, in arguing that because modern psychology has points of common ground with the Torah, they must be basically compatible. Nothing can be farther from the truth, be it ever so uncomfortable to those who search for an easy reconciliation of diverse disciplines. Psychology and the

Torah answer the question "What is man?" in far too divergent a manner. For all of these reasons I look forward to a large number of critical inquiries from readers in search of further clarification.

It is with pleasure that I can offer partial repayment to some of the many people who assisted in my work by hereby acknowledging their good will and expert advice.

To my father-in-law, Chaim Nussbaum, rabbi, Torah educator, and atom physicist, I owe many hours of inspiring conversation, and the frequent, gentle reminder that the time had come to write something down. His uncanny ability to see the issue behind the words is one of his many qualifications for intellectual leadership.

Dr. Dvora Levinson, Coordinator of Child Assessment and Counseling at the Institute of Child Study, proofread the first three chapters with great care. She raised some important questions, and her learned opinion was a good forecast of future reactions to the book.

Dr. Cliff M. Christensen, Chairman of Applied Psychology at the Ontario Institute for Studies in Education, discussed some of the contents with me. As one of his former students, I appreciate the personal encouragement which never seems to falter.

Dr. Micheal F. Grapko, Director of the Institute of Child Study, has provided a congenial working environment during the years it took to develop the ideas in this book. His personal support and warm encouragement were constant.

Ms. Barbara J. Brodie must be singled out for her fortitude in retyping rough drafts with poor legibility. She really worked beyond the call of duty.

Joel Klein

Toronto, Canada
November, 1978

PSYCHOLOGY
ENCOUNTERS JUDAISM

CHAPTER I

On the Conflict between Applied Psychology and the Torah

INTRODUCTION

This chapter is written in reaction to a trend of opinion expressed by various authors (Bulka, 1976; Spero, 1976a) which would lead one to believe that the discipline of psychology and the principles of the Torah are easily reconcilable because they are fundamentally not very much at variance. Nothing can be further from the truth of the matter. Anyone who has accepted some of his training in the thought paths of the Torah can only be startled upon his first introduction to the world of psychology, all the more so if this experience is transmitted not only via books but through the living environment of a university world which ceaselessly confronts one with alien ideals. These conclusions will be demonstrated through a brief history of recent systems of psychology and by a description of important ways in which the challenge of psychology to the Torah differs immensely from the challenge of the physical sciences. These remarks will be confined to the applied areas of counseling, clinical and school psychology which I have studied intensely for the past ten years. Although my personal bias as a former Yeshiva student is no doubt reflected in these arguments, it is equally honest to state that I have approached the social sciences with the belief that it represents one of the most noteworthy modern demonstrations of an intellectual phenomenon whose fabric is inextricably enmeshed with truth and falsehood. As such its discoveries cannot be wholly accepted or rejected, but a thorough understanding of it is necessary if correct decisions are to be made concerning the practical utilization of its resources.

The Historical Background - Psychology as a Science

The tenor of 20th century psychology in North America was strongly determined by the 19th century laboratory of Wundt, a German psychologist with many students. Wundt viewed psychology as an experimental science separate and independent from the philosophical study of man which often characterized European psychology. Today the major claim to scientific status which psychology can make is through its statistical method. The continuous improvement of research design and the increased sophistication of statistical methodology now make it possible to ask questions which previously had to be set aside as desirable but unanswerable. Paradoxically, at the same time that these advances have been made, a number of issues have been raised which have bred a growing skepticism about the scientific exactitude of psychological data. A touchstone of scientific respectability in the biological and physical sciences is the replicability of any experiment. It was once common practice in graduate schools to accept a replication of a famous psychological experiment as a suitable study for a master's thesis. To almost everyone's surprise, the results were consistently divergent in so many instances that such a proposal is no longer acceptable to a thesis committee. It is now understood that many experiments including those of recent origin cannot be replicated. Is psychology then a science? The professional reaction to this dilemma is to explain the lack of experimental replicability with human subjects as an accurate reflection of the endless diversity produced by social, psychological, and economic factors.

Another less generous response to the dilemma is the quiet suspicion that psychological experimentalists are less than thoroughly scrupulous in the conduct of their enquiries. The most extreme example of probably outright falsification of data, one of scandalous proportions on a most serious topic with ethical implications (Kamin, 1974), is the exposure of the defects in Cyris Burt's (Rensberger, 1976) data on intellectual assessment. When it is realized that this major figure in British and American psychology was the first psychologist to be knighted, and was the recipient of the Thorndike Prize of the American Psychological Association, no one but a person with an iron determination to remain naive can view the reported results of psychological research as thoroughly trustworthy. In fact, the current trend among my colleagues is to treat published articles of research as topics for intellectual arousal which engender discussion and lead on to other questions of investigation. There is no closure on any topic.

What is now to be judged of Wundt's hope for an experimental science of human nature? He succeeded but not as fully as he hoped. Psychology today stands between philosophical essays of European flavor relying on logical operations developing stated assumptions and appealing to the face validity of the arguments on the one hand, and rigorous experimental exactness on the other. For the weight of many experiments on a given topic does produce sufficiently consistent data to allow for a few valid generalizations to be made. Alas, the emergence of fixed laws of human behavior is nowhere in sight, and the field is full of small-scale theories which are so loose that it is the common sport of sophisticated academicians to explain the data supporting one theory with the constructs of a diametrically opposed theory.

In view of these problems, how can the scientific discoveries of psychology compare with those of the more established sciences? Can its data, let alone its theories, be seen as anything more than springboards for active speculation about the human condition? Then why are its proposed discoveries accepted and defended by the public with greater tenacity than the hard core data of physics? Although psychology still promises more than it can deliver, one cannot deprive the public of its will to "believe in psychology" as I learned from my experience as guest lecturer to adult groups. Nothing less than a wholehearted support of its claims will quieten an audience distressed by a more scholarly and balanced view of the discipline. The weight of the challenge to the Torah by psychology is given its main force by public opinion operating in defiant disregard of the facts.

The Systems of Applied Psychology — Freud

No one can record the direction of modern psychotherapeutic intervention without describing the influence of Freud, although his contribution can be more briefly treated on the assumption that its main features are faily well known.

Freud (1920, p. 167-168) accepted certain assumptions about determinism in the physical sciences and by loose analogy applied them to mental phenomena. He never believed mental events could be predicted because it was not possible to know all of their antededent causes. Physical determinism however remained theoretically true in his opinion. By believing a person's decision to be caused by a multitude of internal factors, many of which lay hidden to the person himself within deep layers of the unconscious, one begins with an explanation of human behaviour and ends with an excuse for it. How culpable can someone be for unknowingly perpetrating some harm? He can certainly not be accused of wilful malice, for in a sense he is not himself, but a conglomerate of forces directing him. Beneficent acts are likewise less attributable to their doer. The Torah itself recognizes levels of conscious awareness in human behaviour and the degree of responsibility fluctuates accordingly. King David (Psalms 19, 13-14) asks of God, "Of unconscious faults, hold me guiltless. Restrain thy servant also from wilful sins; let them not have dominion over me, then shall I be blameless." But ultimately the principle of free will, a very foundation of Jewish thinking, makes the claim that a person can control and overcome the various psychological forces that affect human behaviour. Man is ultimately answerable for his actions. Although it has been argued (Klahr, 1976) that it is more the cult of dogmatic scientism than professional science that is in conflict with the Torah, this cannot be claimed of the science of psychology which grapples with the question "what is man?" It is not similar to a certain interpretation given to a discovery of science, like fossil evidence, that contradicts one of the many claims of the Torah. The confrontation is in a sense more fundamental since the theoretical formulations of a major portion of applied psychology are erected on assumptions which ask you to accept a portrait of man which is alien to the more lofty and noble claims that the Torah makes for him.

At the same time there is a great divergence in psychology between the theory and its practical consequences. Despite the theoretical complexity of Freud's system of psychoanalysis, psychiatrists actually spend a lot of their time whittling away at the client's conscience. Assuming that the client suffers from neurotic guilt over things for which one is generally not held responsible, the therapist finds in the theory of mental determinism a convenient tool for therapeutic progress. Unfortunately, guilt is not easily eradicated; yet if all practitioners fail in their ambitious goals, it must be admitted that some are successful in reducing neurotic anxiety in a few of their clients. The obvious question then becomes what criteria are used to differentiate normal from neurotic guilt. Are feelings of self-doubt and torment aroused by the disposal of a sickly parent in an old age home, instead of caring for him at home with much inconvenience, an example of reasonable or unreasonable anxiety? In a moment, all of the moral conflicts of mankind are thrust before the therapist for his decision. And at this point the system moves even farther from its theoretical mooring and counseling becomes the counselor's decision as to what he considers appropriate goals for the client. Despite the innumerable positions one can take towards these ethical issues, the general approach of applied psychologists is very similar to Freud's. He believed that much stress in Western civilization was caused by sexual repression. Some leaders in the field admit openly to procuring sexual partners for their clients as a "therapeutic variable" when other approaches have failed. In a recent survey (Holroyd & Brodsky, 1977) 5% of clinical psychologists in the U.S. claim to have had intercourse with their clients. While the latter practice is contrary to the ethical codes of psychologists, a lot of behaviour which the Torah would label unadvisable, such as touching or caressing a dis tressed client, is part of widely accepted clinical practice. In addition to encouraging sexual expression, therapists are fond of promoting defiance to authority figures in the client's life. Little recognition is given to the Torah system of belief in which parental authority is central to the perpetuation and continuity of a set of values. The less children respect their parents, the weaker is the iden- tification with their goals in life. These are some of the shocks that eager orthodox students receive upon begin- ning their university study of applied psychology. Any Jew who enters the field will soon see himself as Abra- ham, with the whole world on one side of the stream and himself on the other. He will have to repeat con- stantly to himself that it is true, the world is moving in one direction and he is moving in another. It may be part of the definition of a Jew in a free society which strongly encourages adjustment to the views of the majority as an indicator of mental health.

Freud introduced the anti-religious attitude into psychotherapy with a vehemence. Arbitrarily he attrib- uted many social problems to religious causes and ac- tively fought against the religious convictions of his clients. These prejudices he recorded with pride in his journals. By establishing himself as the model for a therapist who uses his personal influence in working against the value system of the client, Freud enabled his followers to do much mischief with a clear conscience. So great was his personal animosity to religious belief, that disregarding historical evidence and the bounds of

9

reasonable theory he published "Moses and Monotheism" (1939/1955). In this book he attempted to convince the reader that Moses was an Egyptian whom the Jews murdered. Against the advice of his friends he managed to produce the most ludicrous serious book of the 20th century.

It is worth noting that 40 years after Freud's death, many clinicians, including those who consider themselves opposed to his theory of psychoanalysis, follow his life pattern so closely that they, like him, strain to overcome the client's objections to their advice for a more relaxed attitude towards sexual acting out. Ironically, many of these self-same therapists would never dream of violating the conservative, middle class life pattern which they have accepted as personally appropriate. To this hypocritical cant of a psychologist I have often been witness.

The conflict between the Torah and psychology is often heightened by virtue of the personality and belief systems of the individual therapist. There are a few therapists who know of the Torah and some of its precepts; nevertheless, they are completely ignorant of the relationship between the Torah and the person who accepts it. Far too often they see it as a bundle of regulations, mainly prohibitive, which surround and constrict a person's life for no constructive reason, the unfortunate result of his being born into such a situation. They cannot imagine that someone would voluntarily embrace these teachings as a preferred way of life. Counselors cannot see the joy which the Torah brings to those who study it, nor the many practical advantages it provides in the conduct of daily living. They do not accept its holiness and are insensitive to its beauty. To the untutored eye it is another form of authoritative coercion, and the game the therapist plays with the client is to show him how to abide formally by the Torah while at the same time sidestep-

10

ping it. When a parent refuses their advice to transfer a slow learning child from a religious school to a public one which has a lighter curriculum because the latter lacks a Torah environment, the psychologists shrug their shoulders in absolute astonishment. "Why should such a consideration stand in the way of the child's adjustment?" they ask. It is a common mistake of members of the profession to imagine that their study of some generalized theories of personality automatically give them the key to understand human life in all its diversity. There is little malice in the psychologists' reaction. The patient is simply beyond their reach because he lives in a different world.

Another way of describing this dilemma is to say that psychologists often confuse could and should. By giving a child an intellectual and personality test, the psychometrician in certain instances can predict with accuracy his academic performance. In limited areas there is justification for a psychologist to claim that he knows what a child *could* do. What a child *should* do with his ability is a moral question and not within the therapist's area of expertise and training. Of the alternatives open to the parent of a slow learning child, one can think of a modified curriculum within a religious school, or a public school education with after school hours of religious studies. It is not the psychologist's role to state what a child should do. Unfortunately, the distinction between could and should is not always honoured.

The Theory of Carl Rogers

Rogers' approach is so fundamental that nearly all training in applied psychology begins with him. Once the student has mastered this approach he chooses either psychoanalytic or behavioural theory as his area of

11

specialization. Despite the chaotic profusion of current schools of psychotherapy, the basis for a student's future advancement is wisely made within this framework.

Rogers (1957) had the courage to state unequivocally what he considered to be the necessary and sufficient conditions of therapeutic progress with all clients. His basic terms are empathy and unconditional positive regard. Empathy is the ability of the counselor to reflect accurately to the client the emotion that emerges from his current conversation. Unconditional positive regard is the attitude of the counselor to the client which reflects that the client is a valuable and worthwhile human being in his eyes. There is ample evidence (Truax and Carkhuff, 1967) that greater client self acceptance emerges when these variables are employed by competent practitioners. These variables are similar to Freud's in that they place heavy reliance on understanding and not judging the client. And who wouldn't experience temporary relief from psychological suffering given a little sympathy and understanding? The implicit message to the client, however, is that regardless of what he is or what he does, he will never fall in the estimate of the counselor. There does not seem to be a more amoral doctrine prevalent today in psychology. Even if one fails at this superhuman task of unfaltering regard, by making it the desirable ideal of professional practice one assures the community of clients that as far as the counseling relationship is concerned there are no recognized limits to their behaviour and there is no question of human accountability, a theme which is central to the Torah.

The Behavioral Approach

During the past 20 years the behaviorists have increasingly challenged the theoretical claims of the Freudians, and have been victorious on a number of issues. They claim to have a more empirical approach to treatment and state that their findings are more firmly rooted in learning theory (Wolpe, 1973). Theoretically, learning theory is more demonstrable experimentally than psychoanalytic theory. Earlier attempts (Mednick, 1963) to test experimentally Freudian concepts either met with negative results in a number of cases, or were indecisive in others. A few key concepts still seem untranslatable into experimental procedures and remain untestable. Pavlov's laboratory, however, provided the behaviorists with a small number of very powerful explanatory concepts such as conditioning and extinction. Although the evidence for learning theory was largely derived from animal experiments, this school of thought advanced the facile claim that man was also subject to learning through conditioning experiences and then deduced that man was nothing but the product of these experiences (Watson, 1925). This is a personality theory which denies very effectively the existence of personality. Its claims are so extreme that many of its followers prefer to call themselves empirical not metaphysical behaviorists.

It is worth noting that even though Freudian and behavioral theories of man are at variance with the Torah, the therapeutic variables they employ are simply facts which in no way support or refute the views of the Torah. Freud used transference, the pointing out to the client that he is now shifting his emotional reaction to other people onto the therapist, e.g., directing to the therapist the anger he feels towards his father. The behaviorists provide a reward for certain acts whose frequency of occurrence they thereby wish to increase. Both transference and reinforcement are visibly effective in some situations and in themselves are not disputable principles. But by acting in compliance with the permissiveness of the age, psychotherapists have used these scientific principles in ways which are very much contrary to the teaching of the Torah. Psychotherapy does not represent a movement independent of current social opinion, but just takes and exaggerates some of the demonstrated public permissiveness, giving it the authority of medical advice. And it is curious to observe practitioners who make the claim of independent thinking when all of their basic decisions have been made in quiet conformity with the tenor of the times.

It appears that if traditional counselors quietly violate ethical principles in the confines of their offices, behaviorists are more public and vociferous in their claims for taking extreme steps in remediating many forms of problems that were earlier shown to be untreatable by traditional methods. As various procedures were singled out on account of their incompatibility with clients' rights such as the inhumane treatment of prisoners (Serber, 1975), it is not surprising that recent state legislation (Davison & Stuart, 1976) has focused on the curtailment or prohibition of the activities of behaviorists. When the theory that gives the least credit to human powers produces the greatest ethical violations, it does not make sense to argue that one can accept certain theoretical principles without being tainted by the malpractices that lead logically from those premises.

But the behaviorists now have their hands full with theoretical difficulties as well. It is becoming increasingly difficult to explain their results in terms of learning theory alone without calling in concepts from systems which cannot be reduced to principles of conditioning; furthermore, the traditionalists have claimed that behavior therapy is often effective because of the supportive relationship established between counselor and client, the gum drops or other token rewards having little to do with outcome. Thus far, no one has been able to design an experiment that would test this proposition.

The Efficacy of Psychotherapy

All of our contentions about the malpractice of psychotherapy and its normative application derive from our attempt to weigh all factors in the balance. How much do we gain and what price do we have to pay for the possible benefits? Until approximately 25 years ago it was quietly assumed that good counseling was helpful while poor counseling achieved nothing. Eysenck (1952) challenged the view that common modes of psychotherapy are effective by putting together some data which indicated that two-thirds of treated clients showed at least some improvement and that the exact number of untreated waiting list clients showed the same improvement. The amount of research this problem has triggered, and the number of working hours put into fathoming the question of personality and behavioral change is of such massive proportions, that any generalization drawn from it is almost certain to be partially false. The following statements are presented with caution and represent the writer's own selective bias in reading through this grand confusion of conflicting conclusions.

Eysenck seems to be correct in attacking therapists for the overstatement of their professional usefulness. Truax and Carkhuff (1963) have clarified the issue by showing that high empathy counselors promote client progress, while low empathy counselors actually make the client worse. Theirs was the first solid evidence to show that entering a therapeutic relationship presents a genuine risk to the client. The average gains of treated and untreated clients might not differ sharply, but among the treated group more improve and more get worse than among the control group. There seems to be no way to predict accurately a client's chances of success before beginning therapy. So much depends on the personality interaction of the client and counselor as well as unknown and perhaps unknowable circumstances, that the status of psychotherapy must be labelled an art and not a science. It appears that the major promise that can be offered the client as a result of successful counseling is the reduction of anxiety. Not much of fixed personal habits, personality style, life values or ways of relating to other people seem to be changed. According to the language of the psychoanalytic school, the deeper layers of personality remain untouched. Since most clients studied to date are university undergraduates suffering from a generalized social anxiety, there is no solid evidence that counseling is effective for the more severely handicapped population, many of whom never request assistance because of fear and the stigma of being a client.

How do these observations affect the balance of the scales? Although the merits of every case must be decided by properly constituted Torah authorities, certain generalizations do emerge. The moral risk of entering a world alien or antagonistic to a way of life it doesn't understand and cannot support is counterbalanced by the possibility of reducing the subjective stress of life. The special case of suicidal threat, often verbalized by adolescent clients, no doubt forms a separate category because it involves the paramount question of preserving life. Curiously enough, counselors will defend themselves when asked about a client who did kill himself by arguing that he would have done it anyway. It is only when the client stays alive that they offer their therapeutic relationship as the cause. But if one is ready to assume responsibilty in one instance, it seems a logical necessity to accept it in the other.

The present trend to constrict the scope of psychological theory to miniature systems has particular significance for the young college student. When advice is sought, it is my practice to reveal what I consider the truth of the matter: that an intensive concentration in psychology at the undergraduate level will not be too expedient if the goal is the broadest liberal arts education. Half of modern psychology is the study of drive reduction and its reinforcement properties, and this helps little as an introduction to the best that has been known and thought about the world.

The Special Nature of Theory in Psychology

In the other areas of scientific enquiry, theories are proposed to explain data. No data in themselves can be said to contradict the Torah, but theories which interpret experimental data can be at variance with some principles of the Torah. And the areas of theoretical conflict have been few indeed. Theories however, are now seen as tentative vehicles to organize information in such a way that they easily lead on to new research. The truth criterion for theoretical validity is no longer accepted. All theories are tentative until replaced by better ones. Since no theory can account for all the data, all theories are in trouble. And it is this poorness of fit between empirical and conceptual reality which renders theories negotiable and stimulates further enquiry.

But how different is the relationship of psychological theory to the Torah. The conflicting views of psychology

17

are all fighting for what is metaphysically true about man. What are their data? It is the wealth of cumulative life experiences for whose correct interpretation the various schools of philosophy have fought for centuries without being able to present overwhelming and irrefutable conviction to a majority of mankind.

This ability for people to look at the same set of data and draw vastly different conclusions about its meaning leads us to a broader understanding of the Torah's concept of free will. It is not merely another theological concept which is necessary if people are to be held responsible for their actions; nor is it formulated in order to suit the logic of certain Biblical passages. Free will operates more fundamentally than in problems in which a choice between two things is to be made. It is man's psychological freedom to determine what are the empirical facts of life which are in need of theoretical explanation that illustrates how basically free will is built into creation. If a person claims to know anything at all, it is only possible through the exercise of his ability to construe some pattern of reality from the undifferentiated mass of sensory data available to him. The smallest idea presupposes selectivity, order, organization and some purpose or meaning which the mind can grasp, and automatically reveals the operation of free will. The Freudians understand the problem of theory when they start with the assumption that the principles of psychoanalysis are true. All of their data merely demonstrate but do not test the validity of their propositions. What they accept as true is further supported by their selective observations of life, and this is their working system for life and therapy. They consider the behaviorists naive in assuming that discrete instances of conditioning trials can support cumulatively a superstructure of a theory for man. In physical science the data remain unaltered as the theories shift their focus on them; in psychology the data themselves are up for negotiation as the theories of human nature vie for what are the data of human experience. Man is created by his view of himself, and any theory deviating from the Torah succeeds just to that extent in creating non-Torah human beings. For this reason we see most scientific debates centering around two major schools of thought. Either light is a wave phenomenon or light is a particle phenomenon. Not so in psychology where any basic text on systems of psychotherapy can easily list 25. In physics theory is being challenged; in psychology man is being created.

The special nature of psychological theory gives it a distinctive history. Although Newtonian physics has been replaced by relativity theory, it is still understood and applied with considerable validity in certain areas of experience. One can read the history of physics, grasp the logical continuity and explain the present in terms of the cumulative past. This type of history does not exist in psychology. Boring's "Sensation and Perception in the History of Psychology" (1942) does a scholarly job of handling the research efforts and theoretical conflicts of the past, and a more comprehensive text is hard to find. But the issues of the 19th century are so difficult to comprehend and the nature of the experiments, especially grasping the usefulness of any data derived from the project, is so obscure, that it remains one of the most difficult and incomprehensible books in the field. How can any present day researcher see himself as the heir to the efforts of his predecessors? The psychology of man has altered so radically as we interpret ourselves differently in progressive ages, that the issues in Boring's history have not been brought to any closure. In fact, most theories in psychology die of neglect.

As with the past so is the future of psychology unique.

The direction of the discipline is not guided as in physics by the logic of experimentation. Rather it is the force of personality and authority that decides what the psychology of the next decades will be. It is clear to everyone that what Albert Bandura considers to be of importance will lead the way for a large segment of the professional group. Psychology is what men like Bandura say it is. This tendency for personality to organize and dominate the field is largely wholesome because without it there would be no agreement about what constitutes the subject matter of the discipline. Nor would there be any concentrated experimental effort to answer a limited number of questions. At the same time there is a growing critical perception of research in leading university departments of psychology. It was once assumed that the rigorous pursuit of experimental enquiry provided internal guarantees that psychology was a field of ongoing self-correction. With increasing interest in cognition and mental events a skepticism about the usefulness of the scientific method in psychology has developed. Some staff members now give themselves a year's pause from gathering publishable scientific data to study the nature of the discipline itself. Kuhn's book, "The Structure of Scientific Revolution" (1970) has further awakened the need to extricate oneself from activity to observe that activity, and the question "where are we going" is being asked with greater frequency.

The Detractors

Bulka (1976) is one author who would heal the dichotomy between psychology and the Torah by showing that the theoretical claims of science and religion overlap in certain respects. By then assuming that psychology or psychotherapy is a science like the natural sciences, he is able to cite the claims that others have made for the rapprochement of science and religion as evidence for the compatibility of psychology and religion. As Bulka says, "The benefits of the complementary relationship between science and religion extend to the relation between psychology and Judaism" (p.3). This contention disregards the universal consensus which relegates psychotherapy to the status of an art not a science, and qualitatively differentiates psychology from other areas of scientific endeavor. Very few central questions raised about psychotherapy have ever been settled by scientific experimentation, and in no way has the scientific method enabled us to obtain the hoped for breakthroughs in our understanding of the key psychological concepts of learning and perception. While it is possible to gauge statistically the amount of error contained in an experiment, the major premises of psychology remain uniformly recalcitrant to scientific rigor.

As a representative of the scientific psychologist who can guide religious enquiry, Bulka's puzzling choice is Maslow (1971), a man who has been rejected by that community of psychologists who demand scientific credibility. Although admiring his personal humanistic philosophy, so constant and fierce has been their refusal to acknowledge his untestable speculations as legitimate psychology, that before his death Maslow lamented his failure to gain many students. What has Bulka achieved by quoting Maslow the philosopher? And what can be gained by discovering the congruities between some aspects of a given theory of psychology and an isolated passage from the Talmud? In spite of the listed similarities, the fundamental differences which separate the two remain.

Spero's (1976a) approach only resembles Bulka's super-

21

ficially. Beginning with an obscure argument, he claims, "In fact, it would appear prima facie that religion and psychotherapy need to be in some degree similar inasmuch as both must purport specific views of human nature, unlike most other technical sciences" (p. 17). One would have thought that if two disciplines address themselves to human nature from theoretically different frameworks, they would display only trivial communalities. And this is precisely what is confirmed by the examples brought by Spero. He lists some generalities which are equally true of other disciplines: that therapy and religion view people with a mixture of pessimism and optimism; that psychotherapy and religion recognize man's dual nature; we are informed by both that people can change, but immediately cautioned that not all changes are necessarily for the good. To prevent us from being misled by these insights, Spero warns the reader that psychotherapy and religion are not one and the same. On the other hand don't imagine them to be two separate camps.

Spero proposes that therapeutic insight and the Jewish concept of viyduy or confession both "entail an opening of secret associations of information hitherto bottled up at great expense to the psychic stability of the individual. Both also involve a moment of revelation or insight which leads to mental health . . ." (p. 22). In weighing the differences between the concepts, Spero is quick to admit an important point: "The goal of therapy is not to bring moral or religious judgment to bear on the confessed material. The goal of therapy is purely relief from tension" (p. 22). This moral distinction is so fundamental that we are forced to confess our wonder at the mind that first observed their similarity.

Filling his pages with examples which illustrate ingenious minor compatibilities and simple major discrepancies, Spero waits for the last page to reveal his true convictions. He states, "More questionable is whether it (psychotherapy) can become a religious belief system, in that its technical aspect could give way to a religious world-view. This can obtain only if psychology has any-thing unique and important to say about God and one's religious need for God. To this point, it has not. Psychol-ogy must be able to respond to religious questions reli-giously rather than psychologically. Psychotherapy and psychology will have to develop a new language. They will have to say that anxiety, for example, is not merely an affect which signals danger but possibly an affective-cognition which signals the fear of loss of God's love" (p. 32). These powerful lines reveal an author who is his own best critic. Spero (1976b, 1977) has forfeited his right to vituperative attacks on Amsel (1969, 1976), a man who like Spero senses the basic irreconcilability of divergent disciplines.

In the final line of the article Spero discloses the source of his dilemma. He states, "The therapeutic hour should be seen as being one well worth accepting at appropriate times" (p. 32). To legitimize this concept before the scrutiny of Torah law he has laboured long, but by con-tending with himself he has laboured in vain.

Spero records one factual error (p. 32). He asks the reader not to condemn all systems of psychotherapy be-cause of the few which contain philosophical assumptions alien to the Torah. A simple frequency count of the sys-tems and their practitioners will reveal that the vast ma-jority are contrary to the Torah's view of man.

For someone determined to discover for himself the meaning of the Torah or the intention of psychology, such endeavors to yoke together two disparate systems may justly be called the sport rather than the business of intellectual enquiry. If the disciplines are so antagonistic as only to be joined by violence of reason or ingenuity of metaphor that distort before they can instruct, this at-

23

tempt to embellish knowledge can no longer be admitted as a harmless amusement. Psychology will have to adopt a totally different direction in order to make rapprochement feasible.

Scientific psychology can be of service to the Torah if instruments of measurement are employed in conjunction with Torah concepts. For example, Hillel said in "Ethics of the Fathers" 2, 6, "The bashful one cannot learn." If the Torah believes that the students' frequent questioning of the teacher is an important aid in intellectual development and that fear of embarrassment hinders such progress, can psychology provide us with the tools to measure how much is gained by questioning and how much is lost by silence? Philosophical psychology too can help us understand in greater depth some concepts of the Torah. Maslow's notion of peak experiences can be used to elaborate on the Torah's distinction between the mechanical and inspired performance of religious obligations. If this is what Bulka means by a coalescence of science and religion (p. 12) few would disagree, since coalescence refers to a given consistency of direction between two otherwise disparate things.

In summary, psychology has not been able to vindicate its grandiose claims to being the science of man. Consequently, its pronouncements must be handled with extreme caution. An examination of the various schools of thought suggests that this discipline has erected insuperable barriers to the Torah view of man, both in the realms of theory and counseling practice. Some of the techniques advanced by the practitioners of psychology such as transference and reinforcement may be of use to the religious therapist. Similarly, the behavioral methods of anxiety reduction can be of practical value if one disregards the theoretical framework and goals of that school of thought. Whether the Torah proclaims its own system of treatment will be dealt with in another chapter.

CHAPTER II

Does the Torah Provide a System
of Psychotherapy?

In the previous essay the author dwelt on the differences between current systems of psychotherapy and the precepts of the Torah. The huge gap between the principles and practices of therapists on the one hand and the Torah ideals of human conduct on the other, may lead one to despair of reconciling the two without doing violence to one in order to make it fit the other. Is it likely that the Torah does in any obvious or direct way state a number of principles which parallel in some isomorphic manner the theoretical inventions of 20th century psychologists? Should one simply dismiss the counseling practices of modern man as alien to the Torah, or can one glean certain techniques that are in accord with the requirements of Torah Jewry which has neglected to delve into this issue until modern times? Is it possible to find in the Torah itself an alternative system which therapists might utilize and from which clients might derive the benefit? In this latter approach the intellectual

25

creations of secular minds are of positive use to the Torah, because without their claims to veracity and acceptability no one would ever have thought of turning to the Torah once again to reveal an aspect of its universality which had long been neglected. If it can be demonstrated that the Torah has always contained the foundations for a system of therapy, then the challenge posed by secular philosophy may become another means of revealing the eternal resourcefulness of the Torah in meeting the ever changing stresses of daily living.

A further preliminary question is whether a life lived according to the Torah would make therapy unnecessary altogether. Since counseling embraces so many different problem areas, it is necessary to give a divided answer on this issue. God created man simple, says Koheles (7, 29), but they sought out many inventions. By implication the complicated plans that man envisions are really not necessary, but just things he seeks out. And the Torah life with its emphasis on family solidarity and its clear cut program for living the good life does obviate much of the confusion and discontent of modern living. Nevertheless, many of the anxiety problems which surround living with other people are fostered in parent-child relationships that employ excessive or unjustified amounts of verbal punishment, or that are too permissive so that they fail to provide a guiding structure for development. In addition there are psychological problems which arise from poverty, illness, physical handicaps, and limited learning capacity which hamper normal personality development and demand special remedial attention.

To open the discussion of the Torah's system of therapy it is necessary to state one major premise that separates it from all current systems—and that is the Torah's belief in the spirituality of man. The directive to work at understanding the Torah and the imperative to fulfill what one has learned, make the problem of healthy and distorted personality development of secondary consideration. By following the precepts of the Torah the individual actualizes himself. Man relates to what he can perceive as holy in life and personality provides the unique vehicle through which such divinity is expressed. As one famous Chasidic leader once said, he would not want to be Abraham because that aspect of godliness which is expressed through his own personality would then remain unrevealed in this world. The Torah counselor is thus faced with a client's psychological problem which prevents the full development of his unique spiritual potential. Personality traits become significant since they are seen as an important means to the ends of the Torah. Scholars have delved deeply into the special qualities of the founders of the Jewish nation. On the holiday of Sukos the Jew enumerates the Abrahamitic quality of kindness, and Isaac's trait of justice. Another dimension of character is added every night concluding in the holiday of the rejoicing over the Torah.

At this point one might speculate that as long as the counselor treats only the personality and not the client's religious belief system, then any counselor who employs competently the known therapeutic variables of a given school, such as empathy or positive reinforcement, will be of service to the goals of religion by removing personal obstacles to the expression of self-fulfillment. Unfortunately, those with experience in the field know that such an outcome is not at all secure. In all honesty one has to tell a religious client that the effects of counseling are unknown to such an extent that quite without the intention of the counselor the client's belief system may be damaged. Although counseling experience does not generally lead to atheism, isolated cases have been reported of clients who defected completely from the goals of the

Torah. Whether incompetent or unscrupulous counselors precipitated the reversal in outlook, or whether the clients used the counseling encounter as an excuse to change their outward behavior in alignment with their already altered belief system, can only be speculated. As long as human relationships remain inscrutable, the risk remains that there may be a causal connection between the counseling process and the loss of Torah values.

The only way a Torah system of counseling can work is when the client and counselor share in the responsibility of utilizing their relationship through an open and explicit contract in which they join forces to alleviate obstacles in the path of the spiritual development of the client. In such a procedure the differences between Torah self-fulfillment and the self-actualizing motive of other theories of counseling become apparent. Although Rogers (1955) and Maslow (1954) differ slightly on its definition, the motive is generally seen as an innate drive towards greater acceptance of oneself and others, i.e., the ability to live life with little guilt, shame and anxiety. Self-actualized people are spontaneous in their thoughts and behavior, and are relatively independent of their culture and environment, although they do not demonstrate their autonomy in a behaviorally unconventional way. They readily detect falseness in others and strive to be genuine and true to themselves. These statements contain the assumption that man is born good and will strive all his life to do good if the restrictions of the social order would only allow him. It unquestioningly accepts certain naive assumptions about the "good man" versus the "wicked society" and presents as little scrutiny of these ideas as did Rousseau, their philosophical originator. The theory of self-actualization is stated vaguely, using loose language, and it is a curiosity that of all the speculations of modern psychology, just this one that has so little documented evidence to support it has gained the most widespread credence.

So prevalent is the belief in the inherent human motivation towards self-actualization, that even those counselors who profess adherence to another school retain it as a silent working assumption. Given the flimsy way its concepts are expressed, it is hard to know how any evidence can be gathered to support or refute the theory. But this problem in which ideas are publicly accepted with no evidence or in disregard of the evidence is an issue in the field of the social science of the intellectual history of mankind and remains beyond the concern of our immediate enquiry.

If we turn now to the Torah, we find that its concept of self-fulfillment is clearly more operational in that generalized concepts are stated through the teachings of the Torah, and specific applications are prescribed through the enumeration of the commandments. In this system self-fulfillment is the spiritual achievement and the healthy personality is the vehicle for its success. This is the higher meaning of being true to oneself.

The notion of excessive guilt is likewise treated in the Torah's system. One should feel ashamed of leading a life far below one's spiritual capacity and legitimate mistakes are to be regretted. Shame over things the Torah does not specify as shameful is useless and damaging and ought to be the object of removal through the Torah's system of counseling. Some people suffer agonies of embarrassment over spilling some soup on a tablecloth. Similarly, we have all seen a poor fellow worried to distraction over the accidental appropriation of some object so small that most owners would be happy for him to have it as a gift. On the other hand a brief slanderous remark whose comic sharpness often draws public laughter is of far greater consequence because many are unaware that it violates the Torah and therefore they never repent of the practice. Without the Torah as a guideline, there would be no way of weighing the comparative seriousness of misconduct. And justified shame is a necessary precondition of forgiveness. A person's faith in God's pardon for genuinely regretted behavior returns him to his previous high standing.

What does the Torah suggest the counselor employ as a means of handling those personality problems which interfere with the client's metaphysical goals? Not the least important is the recognition that the client is something more than his personal traits and characteristics. What one feels for the moment is just another consideration to be managed in relationship to other life goals. But more directly the Torah counselor can learn much of his professional behavior from an adaptation of certain insights provided by Ibn Paquda in his difficult book, *Duties of the Heart.* To the extent that I grasp them, I have taken the liberty of translating some of his central concepts into modern terminology. As a psychologist, Ibn Paquda seems to be saying that the source of religious interest as well as its perpetual maintenance is the feeling of joy that one receives from being alive. The greater the pleasure one derives from the daily experience of his life, the stronger are the foundations for religious devotion. No one can formulate a notion of God and wish to establish a relationship of service to Him, if this relationship is not understood to be reciprocal. If a man wants to base his religious life on the idea of a sacrifice in which he gives all and gets nothing, such a plan is destined to failure from the start. Religion, according to Ibn Paquda, can only begin after man is aware that he has received something pleasurable from a heavenly source. Through logic or training, this perception prompts a desire to requite good for good. And the service of recompense must itself produce pleasure. Bound on all sides by the conscious sensation of pleasure in his flesh and spirit, a Jew is ready for the Torah. Nothing is as antagonistic to this process as the daily experience of purposelessness and dejection, or the paranoid suspicion that dark forces operate in the world to induce undeserved suffering. And nothing promotes this wholesome development so much as a childhood saturated with the delights of existence, as the Psalmist (90,14) declares, "Satiate us with your kindliness in the morning (of our lives) so that we can rejoice for all the rest of our days."

Some of these contentions can be supported by Halacha (Law). It is commonplace to quote the rule that the court can force a father to hire a teacher for his son. This can easily lead one to conclude that coercion is a way of the Torah, and that the pain of coercive pressure is consonant with the Torah way of life. But nothing is farther from the truth. A court can force a father but the father cannot coerce a teacher to teach nor can anyone coerce a student to learn. The act of learning is always preceded by an inner decision to allow oneself to change in the direction of the information to be presented. One must make an internal decision of intentionality in which one regards new learning as personally relevant, to be absorbed and united with oneself. This is expressed in one of the first verses a Jewish child is taught, "The fear of God is the beginning of wisdom" (Psalms 111,10). A prerequisite to learning is an attitude of respect to what is to be learned. It is in fact impossible to imagine how one can force meaningful learning through the use of external pressures even in instances where the threat of great suffering is employed. The Sages specified that one should always learn what his heart desires and this is taken to be a positive injunction, not just good advice. And joy is used as an index of achievement in learning Torah. The

31

greater the understanding, the greater the joy experienced and the greater the union of God, Torah and the Jewish people. Pain and coercion are antithetical to this entire process. When the Torah forces the father to hire a teacher for his son it is because he himself is not fulfilling the precept of "teaching the Torah to your son." This deprives the child of life and happiness.

The next step for the Torah counselor is to discover means by which the client's sense of pleasure can be elevated. Good Talmudic teachers have always grasped these principles intuitively and applied them with great conscious direction. Since the Torah had to be studied and lived in everyday life, they were concerned not only with the academic progress of their students, but with total personality development, making them counselors as well as teachers. Some flooded their students with an overwhelming sense of their personal importance, not only through a learned discussion of the Torah's estimate of the worth of an individual soul, but through their own personal relationship with the student. The deep respect for the student is expressed by Rav Chanina (Taanith 7a): "Much have I learned from my teachers, and from my friends more than from my teachers, and from my students more than from all of them." In this manner the teacher was himself living proof of the Torah's valuation of the student, and one could easily feel the truth of one's worth as the embodiment of virtue is expressed physically and emphatically in the person of the teacher who is supposed to exemplify the constant striving for spiritual perfection. The teacher had to love human nature greatly and be deeply sympathetic to the requirements and feelings of the student before the latter could discern God's image before him. Clients are sensitive to counselors. Opinions expressed without a concomitant sincerity have little effect. The outcomes of such a Torah counseling encounter is thus determined by the counselor-teacher personality much the way it is in secular counseling. And it is difficult to specify who will succeed as a counselor. All we know are the happy products of such a relationship after the teacher had demonstrated what he can do. Attempts have been made to train counselors to increase their expression of empathy and concern, and some success has been reported (Matarazzo, 1971). Such training packages are available and it might be a worthwhile experiment to see if those teachers who submit to a brief training program produce students with a greater desire to learn.

Another aspect of the personalities of the famous teachers of our past is the buoyant sense of optimism and hope which they reflected. Since Jews are the prisoners of hope, (Zechuriah 9,12) it is worth studying the subject in detail. Those giants who led the people with greatest strength were men who derived from the Torah their quiet yet firm conviction of the beneficent forces which shape those aspects of our lives which lie outside our immediate control. Their presence projected hope on to those who followed them. Fears of all sorts were forgotten. And it has been demonstrated that those counselors who reflect fear and anxiety themselves are among the least successful.

Hopes are often not fulfilled, and this is ordinarily taken to explain the meaning of "prisoner of hope"—someone who remains dutifully tied to hope in spite of the continued appearance of unhoped for consequences. But a deeper analysis of the phrase shows it to be another divine command to enter a pleasure producing relationship with the world. The act of hope is itself pleasurable, and perhaps more to be enjoyed than the realization of the hope. Disappointments, we are taught, should not be allowed to alter the delightful state of hopeful feelings, for only through delight can we see God.

If it is difficult to change who you are, it is easier to change what you do. Simple reward programs can be established between a counselor and client much the same way they are for a teacher and a class. A contract is specified in which a client receives rewards for certain behavior, just as students in a class can receive check marks or tokens for effort in their school work. This utilizes the Talmudic principle of starting with the wrong motivation in the hope that it will eventually lead to behavior with the right motivation. As simple as this procedure appears, there are common pitfalls which must be obviated by prior training. It is effort that is rewarded, not achievement; rewards must be given without great delay and be meaningful and exciting to the recipient. Lack of effort should not be punished by removing rewards already earned, but other rewards that will motivate effort should be discovered.

To summarize the different perspectives on self-actualization, it is fair to state that secular theorists see genuineness and independence as ends in themselves, whereas the Torah views these traits as means to the spiritual goals of life. If the Torah demands dependence, such as needing nine others to form a quorum of 10, then the client's ability to accept this demand is a vital part of self-fulfillment. When independence is demanded, such as supporting one's opinion of the meaning of a Talmudic passage, the student's life progresses if he is sufficiently strong to accomplish this act of independence. The Torah not only allows for but demands the greater cultivation of various aspects of personality, and cannot consider the achievement of fixed personality traits like independence and genuineness as a pinnacle of development because it reduces the flexibility of the person in handling the diversity of human events to best advantage. This is reflected in their dictum that righteous people have their hearts (emotions) in their control. Personality utilizes and translates human experience as part of the God-man relationship, and it accomplishes it with acts of intentionality. The whole world is worthy of him, as it states in Ethics of the Fathers, (6,1) of one who understands the function of intentionality. Whatever he meets with in life is given meaning and purpose through some aspect of his very diversified personality. Jewish children are forced to develop heterogeneous personalities because the Torah prescribes different behaviors at fixed times. One cannot feel and act on Purim as he did on the fast day before Purim and both of these days are separate from the additional day after Purim and the ordinary day before the fast. The way in which the Torah's concept of time has ensured the rich cultivation of human feelings and elaboration of personality from shapelessness to form and direction enables us to say that much of the modern study of personality development does not apply to Jewish children who require their own theory of development.

If great personal heterogeneity is a prerequisite for full religious life, it might be thought that complexity of form and subtlety of trait inter-relatedness is an ideal of the Torah. Upon closer inspection this is shown to be an error. There are many verses in which the existence of single personality traits unfettered in their isolated expression is considered most desirable. God created man simple, says Koheles (7,29), but they sought out many inventions. By implication the complicated plans that man envisions are not a necessary part of existence, but just things he seeks out. The original intention for man was a simple state in which numerous forces of personality functioned in purity, isolated from one another. Similarly, Isaiah (58,6) describes the work of redemption as an opening of the knots of wickedness. God's goodness is direct, obvious and expressed singularly, whereas wickedness is the result of a conglomeration of intentions which makes life needlessly complicated.

The Torah counselor then has as his goal the simplification of personality complexity. He may employ a system of reinforcement to focus the client's attention to one aspect of his own behavior which then becomes clarified through attentive inspection, or he may reflect and empathize with the client's divided motivations so that the client gains a greater understanding of his own complexity as it is reflected in the speech of the counselor. Occasionally a massive feeling of the pleasure of accomplishment may drive a student to greater diligence at learning, automatically forcing competing motivations into the background. The paths open to the counselor are many, but the one evidence of his success is the client's more elemental expression of his personality in everyday life.

It is now necessary to consider those commandments of the Torah which direct the conduct of social living, such as not to hate your neighbor in your heart, to love the stranger, and not to transmit slander. Indeed, "Love your neighbor like yourself" (Leviticus 19,18) is one of the foundations of the Torah. In answer to someone who asked to have the entire Torah briefly explained to him, Hillel quoted this verse. There are two aspects to it. One is to act kindly to your neighbor, and the second is to act kindly to yourself so that it will be easier to treat others just as well. A great rabbi once visited a wealthy miser infamous for his inhospitality. When he saw the miser eating a dry crust of bread, he encouraged him to eat a more luxurious fare. The rabbi later explained to his curious students the reason for his show of concern and unusual preoccupation with the trivial details of the miser's menu. If the miser has no heart to spend money for his own pleasures, how can he appreciate the needs of others? But if he learns to love himself he might be led to love others as well.

The social commandments are among the most difficult to fulfill because they assume a very high level of personality development. Among people with social anxieties and complex personalities they are notoriously neglected. How can one integrate these precepts into a theory of Torah counseling? On the one hand it is possible to view them as ends of the counseling process. As a result of the counselor's employment of therapeutic variables, the client is free to achieve some of the highest human goals of social living. Anxiety formerly generated by closeness to people who served out large portions of verbal criticism is now reduced by a current closeness with a counselor whose function is to reward conduct and increase the pleasure of social contact. The client who is now aware of how many of his needs are being gratified by other people, enjoys the reciprocity of returning the kindness.

But it is also possible to view the laws of social conduct as means by which the client is brought to a more pleasant personality disposition. It is hard to imagine happiness in isolation, and it is established fact that people who report themselves as experiencing frequent elevated moods are those whose social activities are numerous. What can prompt others to reward a client more than his observation of the social commandments? Keeping the Torah is itself a healing, although it requires an advanced faith and dedication to its precepts to overcome the cognitive misconceptions of social life that clients frequently harbor as a result of punitive childhood experience. They withdraw from it in the belief that it can provide no pleasure, or they despise it as a former enemy. Leaning temporarily on the counselor's faith or trying by small steps to experiment with the possibility of social pleasure, are all methods of making a beginning. In this manner the facts of life are not altered, nor does one ever change the people who encouraged the development of a needless fear of social encounter, but a new understanding of those events are formed along with a freshly established relationship to them. The most common mistake teachers make in implementing these social prescriptions is forcing the student to give in a situation in which he feels he has not received. This concept of self-sacrifice is alien to Jewish notions of the beginnings of education as a reciprocity of deep warmth and gratification. And even an adult can stand at the beginnings of his social education.

The foregoing discussion emphasized the centrality of joy and self-esteem in the normal development of the Torah personality, and some common impediments to this goal. But how does the Torah view more serious mental illness? Sometimes sin is seen as a cause of mental disorder, and sometimes it is psychological difficulties that cause moral error (Wikler, 1978). The case of King Saul illustrates both phenomena. As a result of his transgression he was punished with "a bad spirit" that he tried to exorcise with music. This evil mood in turn triggered occasional outbursts of murderous aggression. Often the Talmud attempts to give a behavioural definition of insanity that it can use as a legal criterion in practical cases. This topic requires a book in itself and for the present purposes psychological problems are defined as a sense of insecurity that leads one to make a dependency response to another person. In fact, intelligent people know how and when to use the human resources around them, and the definition removes the stigma of "being crazy" by going to someone who takes a fee for his services. Most counseling generally is done free of charge by any human who accepts the responsibility of another's dependence upon him.*

If one views counseling as a learning process in which the counselor is a teacher with a heightened sensitivity to the psychological status of his student, then the world has always recognized the place for good teachers. In fact, much counseling has turned in just this direction. The counselor and client isolate a small number of limited problems which the client solves with the counselor's tutorial assistance. Unless the counselor is thoroughly permeated with Torah values, he will be unable to re-mediate the problems of a religious child without damage to his value system. And secular counselors are often un-aware that they have much to learn from the Torah.

*No doubt there are examples of the indiscriminate use of external supports in facing the difficulties of life, and school principals as a group succumb to this affliction more than others. Parents give the charge of their youngsters to the hands of educators who often feel overwhelmed by the problems of recalcitrant learners, behavioural de-linquents, and physically handicapped children. In desperation they relinquish the responsibility the parents have given them into the hands of specialists such as psychologists who often fail of their prom-ises. The specialist has done his best, the principal feels he has done his duty and the poor child is just where they found him. Such princi-pals are better classified as administrators than educators. While some principals have of necessity relinquished their goal of constant per-sonal contact with the student body, they have erred in the transmis-sion of their responsibility to others without any stipulation of accoun-tability. If the activities of a specialist are not monitored and measured periodically so that what is promised and what is delivered can be compared, the child is left with no one responsible for him.

CHAPTER III

The Concept of Personality in Psychology and the Torah

One of the foundations of modern psychology is the belief that theories of personality can describe the behavioural predispositions of an individual at a given point in his life history. Although the concept of personality has been given numerous definitions, most personality theories attempt to account for the individual differences that we observe in those around us. One major area of psychological research has been directed to determining whether such differences between people are stable over extended periods of time, and if so, what casual factors can account for such long-range stability. In this chapter a brief outline of the major approaches to the theory of personality will be presented. This will be followed by a comparison of the way certain Torah approaches handle the same problems.

It is noteworthy that the theorists who attempt to explain the motivational basis of human behaviour start from widely different assumptions although each claims

41

the force of face validity to support the obvious accuracy of his perceptions. As a brief example of great contrast, we see that to Freud sex and aggression are the instinctual drives which propel human behaviour from the first to the last breath of life. These needs cause tension and serve as the ultimate cause of all human behaviour. On the other hand, ego psychologists such as Maslow find a self actualizing motive as the stimulus for activity. Freud views the satisfaction of bodily needs as the basis of human development, and Maslow, looking at the same life data, concludes that the satisfaction of physical strivings is just the early goal of a motive that leads quickly on to intellectual and spiritual fulfillment. Although personality theory poses the question, What Is Man? there is little agreement among psychologists about the answer.

Of course, it is only worth considering these viewpoints if there is some experimental evidence to support the various theories, all of which assume that a description of a personality trait is correlated in at least a mildly positive way with observed behaviour. In fact, do people who score high on measures of aggression or altruism or neuroticism act in accordance with their hypothesized internal motivational states? The voluminous evidence on this point is summarized differently according to the taste and theoretical disposition of the individual critic. Ausubel and Sullivan (1970) review the work on traits such as activity-passivity and achievement motivation to discover an unequivocal positive trend in long term stability. They consider it a good explanation for the continuity of the sense of selfhood through time, and use personality theory to account for the resistance of the individual to rapid change with the fluctuating influences of the environment.

Mischel (1968) presents a useful contrast to Ausubel and Sullivan. Reviewing the same data, he concludes that stability and internal consistency can be demonstrated, but only for intellectual and cognitive traits. Thus IQ scores tend to remain the same on retesting after a two or three year lapse and a person scoring well on one cognitive task tends to score well on another. For dispositional tendencies, such as attitudes towards authority and peers, much lower degress of internal consistency were discovered. Attitudes of Air Force personnel toward father, symbolic authority and boss, bore almost a zero correlation (Burwen & Campbell, 1957). And it is well known that the longer the peroid of time between a test and a retest, the progressively smaller the correlation.

The useful work of Hartshorne and May in 1928 is becoming of great current interest. They tested thousands of children by exposing them to situations where they could lie and steal. Their results showed that moral conduct was inconsistent, although the children's self reported opinions about moral issues were highly consistent. If children were given the tests in different social settings such as home, classroom or club meetings, the correlations of their scores among situations was low. The researchers concluded that children vary their behaviour to suit the situation and do not possess a generalized code of ethics. The responses of the children were so dependent upon given particulars of the situation that even a slight change such as crossing out A's and putting dots in squares was sufficient to change their moral behaviour.

Allinsmith (1960), working with teenage boys, inferred their moral feelings using a written projective test about various forms of immoral conduct. The study concluded that a person with a generalized conscience is a rare phenomenon indeed.

A final note of difficulty is introduced by the general observation that even when more stable traits such as aggression are measured by projective personality tests, there is little relationship observable between scores when more than one test for the same trait is administered. Faced with this core problem in the mechanical procedure of psychological research, many psychologists have concluded with some degree of cynical asperity that psychological research teaches one about research, not about people.

Although the Hartshorne and May data were available 50 years ago, they had very little impact on the psychologists' will to believe that traits were generalizable. Since that time much corroborating evidence for the behavioural specificity of personality measures across situations has been collected. It is fair to conclude that the optimisitic review of Ausubel and Sullivan is receiving less widespread critical acceptance. If self-report measures are notoriously consistent over lengthy periods of time, the cause lies not within the "personality structure" of the individual, but in the stability of his environment which repeatedly presents the same set of stimuli that elicit the same set of well practiced responses. The trend of psychological speculation to date now answers the question, What Is Man?, by pointing to the complex interaction between three sets of variables—individual differences, the specific environmental situation he is faced with and the repertoire of verbal, behavioural and physiological responses at his disposal. The peculiar manner in which these factors interact accounts more for behaviour than any one of the three considered in isolation.

The theories of personality were originally established to account for the uniformity in the conduct of an individual, and since psychologists were interested in predicting behaviour they fitted well with the working assumption that free will was a gratuitous concept. While many researchers might have privately accepted some belief in the freedom of man, as long as psychology wished to design itself along the model of physical science, predictability and the absence of freedom were necessary assumptions. As the evidence against human uniformity mounted, psychologists held on to the hope of formulating a science of behaviour by changing their approach to this end. Personality types were rejected and an interactional theory took its place. While little progress has been made in mapping the ground rules for the way in which multiple factors interact to produce orderly categories of responses, the history of psychology cautions us against excessive optimism. Clark Hull (1952) made a monumental attempt to construct a logically exact theory of learning using the simplest terms of stimulus and response. The increasing difficulties he faced in accounting for a rat's limited behaviour in a maze resulted in mathematical equations of such staggering complexity that it required great intelligence and diligence to grasp it. Confronted with such staggering difficulties in correlating theories of personality to actual behaviour, the field remains in a state of flux. Almost before anyone faithful to the Torah could scrutinize the challenge of personality theory to the traditional Jewish concepts of man, the theory has been partially repudiated and significantly altered by its creators.

When turning to the Torah in search of parallel formulations, we are met with a widely discrepant approach. Everywhere in Biblical and Rabbinical thinking the moral nature of man is emphasized. During the national calamities preceding the destruction of the Second Temple, the populace kept asking each other, Why is the country being destroyed? Their answers demonstrated their conviction that nothing of significance can occur without a moral cause. Everything from political events to transient atmospheric disturbances was related to the moral state of the nation. On a personal level, the Talmud admonishes the individual that when misfortune strikes he must first scrutinize his actions to ensure that he has not been guilty of some wrongdoing. Rav Huna (Berachot 5b) had 400 barrels of wine that went sour. His colleagues gave him this advice:

"Check your behaviour."

"Am I suspect in your eyes?" he enquired.

"Should we then suspect God to punish without cause?"

"Well then," said Rav Huna, "if anyone knows something about me, let him say it."

"We heard," they said, "that you don't give your tenant farmer his lawful share of twigs."

"But he steals much more than his share and I am just retrieving a part of what he has stolen."

"This is the meaning," they replied, "of the popular saying: One who retrieves from a thief also tastes of the sin of theft."

"Then I will give him the twigs," he promised them.

Some say the vinegar turned to wine, while others claim that the market value of vinegar rose to that of wine. This process of self-examination is often cited as an example of the ideal way the people lived the Torah. Man is charged with certain tasks, given free will to execute the appropriate decisions and held accountable for the degree of willful deflection from the path that was within his reach. Whether a man was compliant or aggressive in his relationship with others becomes of interest as it promotes or hinders the fulfillment of moral law. The Torah never sought the abolition of personality as an ideal. It is emphasized that the prophets in their states of transcendent communication never relinquished their high degree of conscious awareness or lost their indentity as individuals. It is through the personality of the individual prophet that his words have greater meaning. The Talmud advises a man with bloodthirsty tendencies to enter the profession of slaughterer of animals. His physical attraction for blood would find there some gratification, and the potential moral danger of his appetite might thereby be averted. The Torah considers the ritual slaughter of animals a worthy deed. Thus the trait itself can be directed for good and evil. Judaism doesn't first inquire about the origin of his temperamental disposition or advise ways in which it can be removed. This is an innovation of modern psychotherapy which is of theoretical interest but at times of little practical utility.

The Ethics of the Fathers is the largest single collection of sayings that bear on the relationship of the personality to the Torah. The moral dangers of anger are specified along with the advantages of having a free and generous heart, and the effect of stinginess on the commandments of charity and kindliness are outlined. This little collection redefines central concepts, turning Western ethics topsy-turvy. Who is wealthy? Someone who is happy with his lot in life. Who is heroic? Someone who conquers his impulse to commit an immoral act. The elaboration of these aphorisms was left in the hands of teachers and rabbis, and certain periods of time were set aside yearly for the study of this work. The custom of fixing times for the public investigation of moral literature is a practice which other legislators have overlooked.

It is difficult to ascertain whether this 2000 year old anthology was accompanied by a mechanical elaboration of moral improvement such as the recording of self-observations in notebooks and counting the frequency of a given behaviour. The Mussar Movement of the last few generations reactivated the public interest in self-scrutiny and moral improvement, and their use of written records as an aid in restraining subjective bias is well known. The basic concern of this saintly group was to break the trait of self-centredness which they conceived as one of the greatest evils of modern society. The story is told of a student who came knocking at a colleague's door late at night. When the colleague enquired, "Who is it?" the friend responded with the word "I."

"Who?" he again asked.

"I," the student emphasized.

The colleague then broke into dreadful lamentation: "There is only one 'I', and that is the one who revealed himself on Mt. Sinai as "I am the Lord thy God!" This preoccupation with breaking the ego ran counter to the liberal individualistic trend of Western society which was more interested in the ego satisfying pursuit of pleasure. This pleasure bias is reflected in many psychological theories of personality which emphasize drive reduction and the ways in which needs are gratified. Much of the Mussar Movement's therapeutic impact to reform deficient nature from its entrenchments in habit and self-complacency was left to didactic preaching, constant self-analysis, reliance on the impetus of faith to break bad patterns, and the hope of reward and fear of punishment. In modern times it would be called a cognitive view of behaviour modification, relying on altered understanding to produce new conduct.

Nowhere do we find the causes of behavioural change codified in the Torah. Not that Jewish intellectuals have been naive about predisposing personal and environmental factors influencing behaviour. The Sages admonished man to keep away from bad neighbours and friends. But these variables have always been considered too complex for specific elaboration. It was this inscrutable complexity of man, which they saw with as much clarity as modern psychologists, that led them to the exact opposite conclusions—behaviour might exhibit certain superficial regularities, but it remained ultimately unpredictable.

People look at the same spectacle of life, but their differing views with regard to man's self-determination creates the most divergent conclusions from similar observations.

The Rabbis were fond of relating historical incidents in support of this point of unpredictability. Hillel said (Ethics of the Fathers 2,5) that one should not believe in himself until the last day of his life. One case used to illustrate this point is that of Yochanan who served as high priest for 80 years and then defected to the Sadducee camp. If personality theory attempts to predict the behaviour of others whom we know less about, Hillel claims that it is impossible to even predict your own behaviour, about which you feel more certain. The descendants of Israel's greatest enemies were among the most prominent teachers of Torah. The grandchildren of Haman taught Torah in Bnai Brak, and two grandchildren of Sennacherib, Shmaya and Avtalyon, taught Torah in public (Gitin 57b). Their conversion and dedication to those ideals which their forefathers wished to eradicate contained no surprise to those who saw every impending moment of life as fraught with the adventure of free will. Certainly between generations no gap was too large to be surprising. Playwrights have long accepted the moral divergence of parents and children as a given phenomenon of life. Shakespeare's "Romeo and Juliet" may be used as a convenient example. Juliet's temperamental and moral disposition varies widely from that of her parents, and yet the playwright saw no cause to offer some explanation. It makes one think that our belief in the indelible influence of early childhood experiences is an accepted but unjustified cliche of modern social science. If in the world of man it is true that "the way the twig is bent so grows the tree," those aspects of human life that can and cannot be thus determined are yet to be specified. It is easy to admit the influence of childhood experience; perhaps free will operates most notably in the direction which this influence takes.

There is one large area of the Talmud which perhaps comes close to the work of personality theorists in its belief in fixed personality types, and that is the concept of Chazakah, freely translated as "we assume" or "it is understood to be so." Chazakah has many legal applications. For instance, in the realm of property rights when the deed is lost the undisputed occupancy on land for three consecutive years provides the occupant with a Chazakah of ownership. We assume, until stronger proof to the contrary is provided, that he is the owner of that land. That area of Chazakah which applies to our current concern is constituted of many Talmudic statements about the nature of man which are predicated on the word Chazakah. For example, "we assume that a man never commits a crime if it isn't for his own benefit." This type of Chazakah has the legal force of a majority. In effect, we assume that the majority of people in such a situation would act that way. The exemplary case is a shepherd who tends a flock. If they are his own animals it is possible that he will allow them to forage on other people's land, thereby committing theft. But if they belong to someone else, he will not allow them to pasture illegally in a field, because we have a Chazakah, an assumption, that most men will not sin unless it brings them some benefit. While the concept is applied legally to a specific case in point, it is accepted that if a doubt arises about the behaviour of the shepherd which can be clarified by self-confession or the testimony of witnesses, then we do not rely upon our legal assumption. Thinkers throughout the ages have nonetheless reflected on the implication of self-interest in prompting a man to violate an ethical regulation. They have accepted the legal rule of thumb as a psychological truism and have fashioned hypotheses from it. If it is true that only some special self-interest can swerve a man from the right track, then it is possible to conclude that the innate desire of man when it is allowed to act unallayed and unimpeded by competing motivations, is to obey moral law. By further implication, one is deceived from his true intentions only by *self*-interest, and the need to act in another's interest is never of sufficient strength to overpower proper action.

A further example of a psychological rule is the Talmudic dictum that in a dispute a man's mind does not lean towards indicting himself (Ketuboth 105b). This generalization provides the reason why judges cannot accept bribes even to acquit those who are innocent and condemn those who are guilty. If a man accepts a bribe he draws close to and favors the donor, making him as his own person, and a man cannot easily discern his own faults. Mar Bar Rav Ashi (Shabat 119a) disqualified himself from judging all cases in which a Torah scholar was one of the litigants, by saying that all such scholars were as precious to him as his own body, and no man could readily indict himself.

This psychological insight is given as a truism which must be accepted as part of the Torah tradition. Likewise, its application to judicial matters is a matter of fact which operates independently of the extent that one grasps its veracity. It is possible to question why it is applied to cases in which the innocent are acquitted or in circumstances in which the judge accepts a bribe from both litigants, but to those who have previously accepted the Torah as their guide to understanding human nature, it provides a system of self-analysis with manifold ramifications. One simply admits that subjective involvements are a necessary part of life, and nothing receives such protective care as the flesh that sits on our bones. We are therefore vulnerable to error in those areas which become important to us through their union with interests. The only protection we have against our vulnerability is the rule of the Torah which shields us from our own weakness. It is understood that all attempts to disengage oneself from this inclination to disregard negative self-evidence will only eventuate in greater self-deception. The remark of Mar Bar Rav Ashi not only illustrates how much he could love a multitude of strangers as long as they studied Torah, but is a self-confession of a great man who could never free himself from subjectivity. His inability to remove himself from the category of the masses of more ignorant people highlights the universality of self-interest, illustrating a certain uniformity of human nature from which different levels of achievement arise.

This system of self-analysis differs from the generalizations of the personality theorists in many significant ways. By citing concrete applications of the insight which have the binding force of law, our understanding of human nature is made deeper and more personally meaningful. It has allowed Jewish thinkers throughout the ages to look askance at the attempts of other philosophers because their ideas were only theoretical, or hypocritical since they were unconnected with life. But the Torah is called a "Torah of Life" because it and the conduct of life are inseparable.

In the system of Freud in which given instincts are postulated as the basic life force which is uniformly influential, it is a long way before we arrive at any high-level generalizations about personality like that of the Talmud. How instincts operate through cultural learning and the particular distortions of individual differences, is so varied in Freud's system, that no truisms about the conduct of life are offered at all. Once a given behaviour has been elicited, it can retroactively be explained by psychoanalytic principles as the result of the operation of various defense mechanisms on instincts striving for expression. But nowhere can their expression be codified because diversity not uniformity is the observable consequence. Almost any behaviour is possible because the balance of internal forces is always delicate and easily shifted by the sudden and unforeseeable introduction of some slight new force which tips the scales of the balance. Ironically, Freud's system begins with physical determinism in the moral sphere and concludes with unpredictability. In a very different light does the Torah see man. Certain things such as the disinclination for self-incrimination are always present at the far end of behavioural causality regardless of the stimulus input. It is a bold claim for the Torah to make that subjective self-involvement has a very specified locus of control of which no man has ever been free. But no one has ever brought evidence to the contrary, nor is the attempt even recorded.

The attraction of Freud's system is that it may be wrong but it is a system. The Torah's insights into personality are not systematized. Jewish sources make numerous references to the personality of man, especially with reference to his inclination to do good and evil. In Genesis 8,21 we read that "the imagination of man's heart is evil from his youth." This seems to imply that man is created at birth with a desire to do evil. Yet in Tanchuma (Genesis 7) we read that a child of five, six or nine doesn't sin, but from 10 onwards his evil inclination waxes. Some commentators, in attempting to resolve this apparent contradiction, have laid the groundwork for a theory of man's personality. But the key point is that the original sources do not. The historical consequence of various endeavors at the construction of systems which often contradict one another, is that each has something to recommend it, but none can encompass the mass of heterogeneous material on personality scattered throughout the sources. Every student of the Torah has had the experience of learning something which he never completely grasped because of the paucity of information presented before him. Years later he chances across the missing conclusion which then illuminates that which was puzzling and hidden. The Torah begins with the axioms that man is created in God's image and has the task of actualizing this godliness through the teachings of the Torah. For all of the wealth of Talmudic literature on innumerable topics, theoretical interests are generally subordinate to the practical goals of living like men—but men as defined from God's viewpoint. Many systems of thought such as practical medicine and statistical probability (Rabinovitch, 1973) can be derived from the Torah by extracting common elements from diverse contexts; the Torah itself rarely performs this exercise because its goals are mainly moral. This taxes the patience of the complacent student who is accustomed to gathering information from an encyclopedia in which almost everything relevant to a topic is summarized in one place and listed alphabetically. It also invites misunderstanding based on partial knowledge.

Most other assumptions of the Talmud are not of such psychological interest. For example, we assume that a man would not engage in an impudent denial of a debt in front of the man who loaned him the money. From the standpoint of personality it teaches us that indebtedness creates a sense of shame in the recipient from which he cannot completely free himself. The major implications of such a generalization are naturally legal and refer to the way demands for repayment are handled by the court. Assumptions are rules of thumb applied to facilitate legal decisions, and not necessarily fixed laws of human conduct. This is further supported by the opinion of the Chasam Sofer (Choshen Mishpat 67) who describes the power of such assumptions as derived from custom.

Thus we can say it is the observed custom of people to act with a sense of embarrassment when confronted by the man who did them a favor. By implication, such assumptions would have no legal force if the custom of a group of people was observed to differ. However, it is of more than passing interest to note that to this author's knowledge none of the prominent assumptions about human behaviour as recorded in the Talmud have been abandoned in the face of changing custom.

In addition to the concept of Chazakah, the Talmud often makes legal decisions based on certain assumptions of human motivation and preference, without calling such generalizations by the name of Chazakah. A case in point is the question of who comes first in receiving money from an inherited estate. If a man died leaving a small estate which does not suffice for the maintenance of his wife and daughters for a 12 month period, who receives priority? The Talmud (Kethuboth, 43a) concludes that a man feels more humiliation when his widow rather than his daughters goes begging for food, and we assume therefore that it must have been his intention to give the money to his widow first, although he never expressed such an opinion. The Talmud is replete with such instances in which an unknown factor is determined by surmising the intentions of people, and the simple justification for such a procedure is that any reasonable person would in all likelihood agree with the conclusion.

Another instance is brought in Kethuboth (28a) with reference to a woman who married, was divorced and remarried. She is not allowed to settle with her second husband in the same courtyard in which her first husband lives. Modesty is the apparent reason for such a regulation. If the house they lived in was rented, she must move away from him. If it belonged to her, he moves; if it belonged to him, she moves. The question then arises about

55

a house that they jointly owned. The Talmudic discussion concludes with Rav's opinion that moving about is harder for a man than for a woman, so she must move. The probable reason for such a ruling is that a man loses his sphere of livelihood by moving from place to place, whereas a woman can secure hers through marriage. We are invited to accept this truism because of the known structure of society which differentiates male from female roles. By implication, such role requirements are not quick to change and we see no legal provision made for possible exceptional cases, since these are no doubt of statistical rarity. Rav's opinion is not usually understood to be the result of his personal observation of life, but the general view of Jewish tradition which he learned from others and transmits to us. It is accepted as valid because it is tradition.

Do these examples indicate that the Torah has its own theory of personality scattered throughout the pages of legal discourse that every now and then relies on what is accepted as universally true about man? If we adhere closely to the psychological definition of personality traits as underlying characteristics, qualities or processes that have a concrete existence and represent relatively stable and enduring predispositions that determine behaviour and can be inferred by measuring their behavioural indicators, then the answer must remain in the negative. Many of the Talmud's excursions into psychology are forms of reading intentions in the absence of more reliable evidence, and kernels of wisdom about the common circumstances surrounding the great human events of birth, marriage and death. They must have considered a general theory of behavioural causality as hopelessly naive in its aim to simplify something irreducibly complex, although they on occasion may have applied single explanatory concepts to isolated incidents in which some motivational factor was obviously operating with great force. One man famous for his righteousness fell into the practice of sexual lust which he pursued in the grand style (Avodah Zara 17a). A coarse joke incidentally coined by one of his partners suddenly brought the moral gravity of his actions to conscious inspection. The impact caused excessive grief and his early demise. In this case a single drive led him to fault, and a singular desire for forgiveness led him to death.

Those who lived in times of religious persecution or political upheaval were naturally more inclined to view life as unstable, attributing causality more to external than to internal events. And finally, they would concur with the modern phenomenological disposition to believe that if you feel free and experience that conviction in your behaviour, then there is no greater proof possible for human freedom. Once this principle of freedom is granted, all theories which view man as passive must be rejected, including reinforcement theory which emphasizes the power of reward to strengthen habits, motivational theory which sees man as inexorably pushed or pulled by drives, and mechanistic theories which claim that responses are simply triggered or caused by controlling stimuli. Not that examples from the Torah illustrating these phenomena cannot be provided. There is the dictum that one should study Torah even for the wrong reasons, for this will eventually lead one to study it for the right reasons. The wrong reasons might include monetary reward or the pride of reputation. It is the sole utilization of such explanatory theories to account for all human behaviour that must always remain inadequate.

Is there a theory of psychology which like the Talmud takes as its basis the common sense view that man grasps reality, can to a certain extent control it, and refers behaviour to underlying conditions of life, formulating them into the dispositional properties of the world? The "naive psychology" of Fritz Heider (1958) comes the closest to postulating the motives of other persons as the major invariant of the environment that gives meaning to what one experiences. Naive psychology postulates that action depends upon factors within the person and within the environment. If we analyze the statements that can be made about a person rowing a boat across the lake, we can say that he is trying to row the boat across the lake, he has the ability to row the boat across the lake, or it is difficult to row the boat 15 miles across the lake. These sentences describe an event with varying degrees of attribution to the person on the one hand and the environment on the other. The concept of *can* and *may* are central to Heider's theory. They are dispositional concepts which refer to relatively stable relationships between the person and his environment. *Can* is defined as the absence of imposed restricting external forces and *may* indicates that another person who has the power over me does not wish me not to do something. If you try you will succeed, and if you try you won't be punished, differentiates *can* and *may*. The theory goes on to explain difficulty as an important dispositional property of the environment, and opportunity and luck as the more variable external factors. Personality traits and attitudes such as self-confidence can critically influence behaviour.

The strengths of Heider's system lie in his choice of topic—common sense observation is a leading source of many hypotheses in scientific psychology and requires delineation for this reason alone. The difficulty with such a procedure is that the vernacular is ordinarily a clumsy way of handling something with scientific exactitude, since many of its terms contain hidden conceptual schemes which are never exposed and examined. Its terms occasionally overlap one another and do not always provide convenient tools for handling experimental data. In addition, the major theories of modern psychology appear to be constructed with the aim of taking accurate psychological knowledge out of the reach of the lay public. Man is exactly not what common sense observation of life would lead one to believe. Freud's system stands naive psychology on its head by claiming that the main energy for life drives is derived from instincts which remain partially exposed but mainly hidden in the unconscious. Since they are disguised by symbols and misshapen by defense mechanisms, the accurate perception of true motives is the royal property of counselors who attained this insight by means of training. Piaget arrives at similar conclusions by his experimental demonstrations that children use words they don't understand and employ conceptual labels they won't really grasp for years. The entire expression of meaning through language is deprived of its substantive substrate. One becomes psychologically famous by demonstrating that things are not what they seem and the arbitrary criterion for the acceptability of a theory is its ability to verify what is publicly held to be false or unknown. To confirm what is believed to be true is the work of an inferior and banal mind.

Heider's theory is primarily one of rational behaviour in which people perceive their environment accurately, and form sound judgments based on the logical use of information. They experience emotions that are appropriate to circumstances and generally choose the right ways for reaching their goals. In the light of the current conflict among psychologists about the role of the unconscious in the direction of behaviour, some psychologists would find many of the foundations of common sense theory arbitrary and ultimately unprovable. And why has Heider constructed a basically cognitive theory if he then goes on to rely heavily on motivational concepts? One cannot hold equal membership rights in schools of psychology which have traditionally seen themselves as antagonistic. In order to explain behaviour naive psychology utilizes close to every major explanatory concept in the dictionary of psychology. We are everything that everyone has always said we are.

A further difficulty of naive psychology is that what is generally called common sense may actually be cultural convention in the field of interpersonal relations. The Talmud apparently equates the two and considers such convention as an inherent part of life's circumstances. To account for voluntary behaviour, naive theory employs many sources of intention: the desires of the individual, his ulterior reasons, the push of sentimental attachments, the propensity to obey requests, follow commands and fulfill moral obligations. When weighing the forces of personality and the environment, Heider will employ one or the other, but not both, to explain the cause of an event. Personality is regarded as significant when the event to be explained is unexpected. Is this a bit of common sense we can all subscribe to, or is Heider recording his own bias and establishing his own convention?

If something is true about man apart from a social system in which he lives, it is hard to imagine how this could ever be discovered, given man's social nature and the fact that an expression of such traits in isolation has never been recorded. We are once again led to the conclusion formulated in an earlier chapter which describes the work of psychology as distinct from the natural sciences. In the former discipline the conventions of social groups and arbitrary language of "common sense" create rather than discover an image of man. And in order to do so naive psychology uses concepts of motivation and cognition in a way that crosses illogically all other theories in psychology. An intention is a private event that is unmistakenly known to the person although it can be successfully hidden from an observer. Such a view partially overlaps and partially disagrees with Freud's emphasis on motivations which are frequently hidden from the person and visible to others. Heider has not freed us from choosing among one of the more limited views of man contained in the traditional theories of personality.

In summary the Torah is concerned primarily with practical guidelines within which its moral and spiritual goals for human conduct may flourish. Generalizations about human nature are mainly made in the realm of law where other evidence is lacking. The practical orientation of the Torah is also evidenced in the way it accepts certain traits such as aggression, bloodthirstiness and selfishness, and suggests ways of using these traits in a positive manner, rather than unrealistically attempting to suppress or alter these tendencies. Only after establishing man's essentially moral nature, his responsibility to his creator and the basic concept of man's self-determination, does the Torah make some generalizations about man's personality. Individual differences are explicable although unfathomable because free will allows for too wide a band of variation. Personality theorists have searched for generalized groups of fixed personality traits that can predict behaviour. That they have failed is no surprise. That they continued in the search after it first became apparent that the approach to the problem needed reformulation is further evidence for the dictum that those who do not understand history are condemned to repeat it.

CHAPTER IV

The Psychology of Commitment
to the Torah

This chapter is dedicated to the many young men and women of our generation whom I have observed thirsting for a Torah life yet at the same time struggling with an uneasiness that arises from many sources. Youth is confronted with a totally divergent world and thought system when suddenly exposed to the Torah. The origin of the word Hebrew was interpreted by the Rabbis to mean one who is across from the others by being opposed to some of their beliefs. He becomes self-consciously aware of the discrepancy between what he has previously accepted as metaphysically true about the world, what he imagined the Torah demanded of a Jew when he had not yet examined the sources, and the final startling statements of the Rabbis as they turned their distinctive pattern of thought to the interpretation of the Hebrew Bible. Examples of the latter will be elaborated in the chapter on the Book of Job.

One common problem is the numerous conflicts that

arise between old ideas that have been accepted as valid and the new ones met with in the Torah. Many of these conflicts are caused by a limited understanding of scientific advances and the naive acceptance of pseudoscientific claims manufactured by the propaganda machine of research. The student new to the Torah often suppresses these questions he cannot answer, or tries to compartmentalize the conflict by wearing two hats. This solution only weakens his commitment to the Torah because it stifles thinking about one's faith, when in fact it is necessary to understand as much as one can about what he believes. The Rambam (Temurah 4, 13) says, "Even though all of the statutes of the Torah are divine edicts, it is proper to ponder over them and give a reason for them, so far as we are able to give them a reason. The Sages of former times said that King Solomon understood most of the reasons for all the statutes of the Torah." Only too often are we influenced by a popular understanding of counseling in which all problems are eliminated before one enters a state of bliss. The Torah claims that problems are a necessary part of the step-wise advancement in our understanding of the Torah, and the process of conflict and resolution which leads to a higher level of problematic knowledge is one of the chief activities of a man in this world. Problems are not to be eliminated even if they could be. One only suffers from a more simple or a more advanced difficulty in his understanding of the Torah.

Frequently does someone caught between these stages of intellectual and emotional progress fail to extricate himself sufficiently from an earlier viewpoint to enable himself to find freedom from elementary forms of skepticism and a desire to hold on to what he was, be it ever so unenviable. Too much of this inner struggle, and I may admit myself as one of these journeymen, seems self-defeating. In searching through the discipline of psychology for some practical advice on how to alleviate this common form of human discomfort, there is little in the half-million articles published a year that might satisfy this need. Much work can be distilled into small observations, and the task of translating such products into something that can be useful to daily living still remains an obscure art. That small part of psychology which appears relevant to our problem forms the subject matter of this chapter.

When a person decides to become an observant Jew he is in effect committing himself to a totally different life style which governs every conscious moment of his existence. The major difficulty to be faced in the consideration of the psychology of commitment is that psychology has no language to handle those forms of behaviours which define the act of commitment. Since such an act is ordinarily described by such words as choice, decision and intention, much that has been written on the subject has been set in the context of existential psychology which has more philosophical freedom though less experimental rigor than behavioural psychology. It is also European in origin and less easily understood by the North American audience. This dilemma will be resolved in the course of this essay by utilizing both the European psychologists for their richness of conceptualization and Skinner's (1972) behaviourism to translate these generalizations into some concrete lines of action. While Skinner has been criticized for maintaining a primitive and oversimplified theory of human behaviour, it is potentially the most fruitful of all approaches to the young Torah idealist. It is unfortunate that Skinner's excursions into psycholinguistics and cultural reform, areas in which his proficiency is doubtful, have triggered a barrage of criticism that has obscured Skinner the psychologist. And so busy are students in trying to go beyond some of his elementary observations, that it is amazing how many professional psychologists holding doctoral degrees know so little of his theory of operant conditioning.

Commitment begins when one is able to perceive oneself as dissociated from the immediate environment. This conviction is necessary to experience a freedom of choice, for if the controls of the environment are all encompassing, a person would never be able to transcend the weight of conformity to external stimuli. After the subjective recognition that the "I" exists apart from its circumstances, it is then necessary to formulate some rudimentary notion of the object to which this "I" will be dedicated. For some people it is the elevating moral law of the Torah and the abundant examples of righteous social living recorded in the Talmud which become the object to which the subject will establish some relationship. For others it is an emotional awareness of God's transcendence and the temptation of establishing an attitude of worship to this object that establishes the goal of their pursuits. For some it is the history of the Jewish people, their current struggle for physical survival and spiritual rejuvenation that becomes the focal point of their interests. And there are those who are searching for meaning and stability in a seemingly meaningless universe. Since the Torah, God and the Jewish people are different manifestations of the same spiritual substrate of life, the pathways to Jewishness are manifold though homeward bound they all lead to the same destination.

The final stage of commitment is that of building a relationship between the ego and the object it perceives. But the subject's mere knowledge of the existence of an object without the concomitant of total commitment is a form of religious training which creates a mutilated distortion of a living relationship. It is a pale shadow of the divine order "to live by the Torah." Commitment, not just observation and wisdom, depends upon an act of the will which propels the subject towards the object and demands a participation in a new, shared existence. One must give of oneself, relinquish part of the separate identity which was a necessary starting point of the process, to allow for the birth of a relationship. The object's recognition of the subject, that step which completes the personal relationship by having the object share in the fate of the subject, is the easiest for a modern Jew to understand and accept. Who can view the course of modern times, see events of such frightening magnitude, and then be still? It is the very piercing perception of God's power behind the destruction of the Second World War that has convinced some people that his presence is not sufficiently beneficent and has weakened their transactional bond to their Creator, while to others it is his very silence which has forced them to consider more deeply the nature of their relationship. The miraculous rebirth of Israel and the restoration of the Wailing Wall have heightened the sense of affirmation and cemented this closeness in a tangible manner.

The commitment between subject and object is defined through their set of relationships and forms a covenant, in much the same way the Patriarchs established covenants with God. Since each party agrees to certain privileges and restrictions that define the relationship, a shared moral responsibility naturally arises which drives each to act with a common scale of values that is the exclusive property of neither. Breaches and alterations of the code are to be expected if the relationship evolves over time, and the phenomena of reconciliation and forgiveness are brought into existence.

To each person there is ample latitude for the expression of his own individual uniqueness within the overall framework of the covenant, but commitment to the

Torah differs from other forms of religious and political commitment because it demands both a behavioural conformity somewhere within the preestablished bounds of the Torah, and an intellectual allegience to a few ideas which can be considered the credo of Jewish life. The hope to build a Jewish life by rejecting the Torah's claim that it contains valuable information about who is the object of our interests and how we go about dedicating ourselves to this object, is to invite self-defeat from the outset. It is impressive to view the wide variety of people who all sincerely claim to observe the same Torah, but there are human limitations to this system of commitment, and the valuation of the Torah as our key to a knowledge of God cannot be sidestepped. Others have tried to force their own illogical twist to obviate the necessity of some intention to believe in its resourcefulness for our purposes, and they have the failure of their own lives and the disappointment in their children to show that it cannot be done. One can waver on the brink between an act of the will and no act, but a third alternative changes the game completely.

Many young people are lonely enough to see themselves as separate from their surroundings, and sufficiently disappointed in the moral state of the world to search for a haven which will extricate them from all their doubts about the meaningfulness of human existence. It is in the definition of the relationship which specifies what is permitted and what is forbidden that the modern problem of faith presides, for inherent in the covenant is a moral responsibility which can only be executed through submission. The very agreement to any principle automatically restricts the subject's degrees of freedom. To a modern audience, submission suggests self-abasement or lowering of self-esteem, and sparks the heady desire to be independent and untrammeled of consequences. How often has an agreement been broken when one party suddenly feels that it violates his own integrity! In order to avoid disillusionment, a young person searching for a home of faith needs to make a studious enquiry of the question of control. And at this point some of Skinner's observations are of relevance.

Skinner is a man who has pondered a long while on the question of human freedom. We leave behind most of the popular works on the subject because they address themselves to the question of political freedom, i.e., under what form of government can a man exercise certain behaviours which he labels as his right of speech, free assembly, vote, etc., and what is the best way of safeguarding these rights from the expansive authority of political leaders. When viewing human freedom on a personal level, it is obvious that we are not free to do things beyond our physical and intellectual capacity. One cannot be considered free to speak French if he doesn't know the language. And we are certainly limited in this moment's freedom by the limitations of our genetic inheritance, the cumulative restrictions of past learning and the rewards and punishments of the immediate environment. It is this last item which is central to our study, because it is the only one within easy reach of alteration.

Skinner is convinced, through data accumulated in laboratory study with lower animals and his own observations of human life, that behaviour is seriously affected by its consequences. Acts which have positive consequences or rewards following upon them, tend to be repeated with greater frequency. Acts with negative consequences or punishments following closely in pursuit, tend to appear less frequently. As simple as this formulation sounds, that's just how powerful it is. It has been my unhappy experience to observe so much unintentional human bungling arising from a disregard of this principle, that I often rejoice that so much more happiness is within our grasp. In assigning grades, it is my habit to give the student the higher one when his performance stands midway between two levels. This practice has been questioned by colleagues who are later silenced by my explanation of this procedure. If one wants a student to continue studying psychology, then reward him for his efforts. If the goal is to reduce the number of hours he will spend on the subject, simply reduce the rewards one offers for past effort. Youngsters are so closely bound to the physical rewards of their environment, that any child-rearing practice that utilizes punishment raises immediate questions as to its validity.

If Skinner is correct in concluding that much human behaviour is lawfully connected to the ensuing rewards, the question of freedom is placed in a different light. One rarely hears a complaint about the lack of freedom when the rewards for slavish behaviour are immense and greatly valued by the slave. In many factories the opportunity of earning double money for overtime work adds considerably to job attractiveness. Skinner's distinction between freedom and the feeling of freedom is pertinent. One feels free when the consequences of work produce pleasure even though the conditions of employment are severely restrictive. Conversely, one feels enslaved when the rewards of behaviour are held in low esteem, despite the very small demands upon which they are conditionally dispensed. Too often we base the estimate of our freedom on a subjective judgement of the rewards without weighing the objective difficulty of the task. People have a curious verbal habit of giving the individual credit for an act if the cause is not obvious. If the behaviour is generally considered reprehensible, the environment is considered to be the cause. Juvenile delinquents often blame their behaviour on city slums. On the other hand, if the behaviour is praiseworthy, everyone wants to see himself as the cause. All of these ludicrous inconsistencies in the way we explain our own lives are the result of an obstinate denial that we are always controlled, at least partially, by the presence of external systems of rewards and punishments. And any counselor who proceeds to help a client by focusing on some internal structure such as an Oedipal complex or free floating anxiety without considering the immediate reinforcement environment of his client at home and at work is headed for serious trouble. In fact, who knows of anyone who counsels that way? Theories of personality are built on the assumed existence of traits which guide and direct the ego through the maze of life circumstances and from these formulations are drawn theories of how to counsel the person caught in the maze. All of these intellectualizations disappear before the potency of the glance of disappointment that twists across the facial expression of a spouse, or the threat of unemployment voiced by a dissatisfied supervisor.

This carefree mode of attributing causality of behaviours solely to internal decisions in merry disregard of the environment is not absent in Jewish circles. A group of people reported on their motives for attending High Holiday services (Lasker, 1971). A questionnaire listed a series of reasons and the subjects in the study simply ranked the items as they applied to themselves. The two highest ranks were given to items that can collectively be called a desire to establish a relationship with God, and the wish to preserve and strengthen one's sense of Jewish identity. So far the results are not surprising. The shock comes when one glances at the group of items that the subjects ranked lowest—the desire to please other people. It is as if those in attendance were unaware that their presence in synagogue had an effect on their friends, relatives, and other people at the service, that was important to them. Since synagogue attendance during the High Holidays is generally rewarded with very strong sentiments of family approval, and spoken of at great length both before and after attendance, how is it possible for people to deny the social nature of their existence? And it must be viewed as a form of denial, for these items ranked lowest because there were no more items left to rank below them. Skinner's answer would be that just these people enjoy less freedom because they to a certain extent are being controlled by factors of which they are unaware, or to which they won't admit. Freedom consists in listing all those factors which delimit our behaviour, either because we cannot be freed from certain necessities or choose by reason of pleasurable preference not to be free from them.

Our arguments lead to a peculiar blend of irreconcilable schools of psychology. There seems to be no alternative to describing a decision to interest oneself in the thought of the Torah without saying that a person is capable of freedom of intentionality, can decide to change the course of his life and succeed at it as well. We employ the psychological determinism of Skinner to make us aware of the difficulties we will encounter in freeing ourselves from the control our reinforcement history exercises upon us, and for certain clues to make the work easier. After one has decided to give the Torah a chance, by placing oneself in an environment that will reward those behaviours he wishes to emit and ignore old patterns he wishes to slowly discard, one can use freedom of choice to persist in the path of his preference. The logic is confusing because we bridge two incompatible schools of thought, but empirically as tested in the conduct of our lives, the results are consistent and satisfying. For those struggling with the problem of self-control, Skinner's ad-

72

vice is refreshing. Just place yourself in an environment that will reward those behaviours you wish to emit, and the burden of internal struggle is ended. By carefully reading through Skinner as he laughs at our naive notions of unlimited human freedom and the all pervasive control of the inner directed man, submission to the covenant loses its demeaning connotation. And if the subject-object relationship is a source of pleasure the whole question of who is causing this enjoyment will fade into the background.

Skinner offers a good understanding of Hillel's warning never to trust in oneself. The Rabbis obviously believed that no form of commitment to the Torah was permanent and inviolable, and if fixed personality traits do exist they account for only a part of the story. Our theory allows us to offer an alternate interpretation of Hillel's statement. When Yochanan viewed orthodoxy as the best means to his reinforcement ends, he professed his allegiance to the Torah. When the Sadducees were lifted in the hierarchy of rewards for which he would work, he switched his allegiance. Both Skinner and the Rabbis might consider this opportunism but neither would describe him as an insincere, duplicitous or hypocritical person. He sincerely meant his roles at the time of their performance. In trying to pinpoint the person we are accustomed by habit to seek for some enduring internal structures of stability, in disregard of the environment. This discussion excludes people who for the sake of rewards say things we suspect they don't mean completely. Such a person was Doeg, Head of the Sanhedrin (Samuel I,21). His hundreds of original legal contributions are traditionally described as emanating from the mouth outwards. He never respected the content of his own speech although he tried quite intentionally to deceive others into believing he did.

73

One last insight into the dilemmas of modern life may be of assistance. If the opinions of the sociologists (Williams, 1960) are taken seriously, one might readily assume that the pressures for conformity are so great today, that much of a person's energies are directed towards avoiding the criticism given to those whose style of clothes or leisure activities deviate even slightly from the norm. And we see people anxiously trying to keep pace with the key phrases of current slang that will be their ticket of admission to the circle of friends to which they wish to endear themselves. On the other hand, a rapid glance through the pages of the daily newspapers would seem to indicate just the opposite—so much freedom is given to individuals as part of their right to "do their own thing" that courts of law, whose choice of decisions includes their interpretation of the public's mood, are increasingly at a loss to decide what degree of unsocial behaviour does constitute a crime. Punishments are imposed leniently because it is now harder to conclude that the accused was not acting within his own rights. But this apparent paradox between the demands for obsequious submission and the acceptance of aggressive independence is resolved when we consider that the former generally applies to those appurtenances of life that are physical and external to man, while the latter can be grouped under the heading of moral law. Today one must repeat some comic phrase exactly as prescribed if laughter is to ensue, though one may violate the laws of inner moral restraint with impudent laxity. This reluctance to declare some act unethical has heavily influenced the decisions of review boards. The number of persons whose registration as a psychologist was revoked for ethical misconduct, or whose license to practice real estate was suspended by a real estate board for unscrupulous conduct, is notoriously small. The public is increasingly doubtful that there is a field of ethics which extends beyond philosophical speculation or a system of fixed values of right and wrong which determines the rewards and punishments of everyday life.

How startling it must be to the young Torah student to realize that this dichotomy is exactly reversed in the eyes of the Torah. There seems to be so little emphasis on cutting different people into the same exterior mold of fashion and wit, and such a serious endeavor to apply a norm of values without prejudice or compromise across all strata of society. As each person formulates his own relationship to God and the Torah, it is the uniformity of observance which creates the unity of the Jewish people. This makes it necessary for one to take a moral stand on certain social issues contrary to the swing of public opinion, and the moral lapses of some systems of psychotherapy which we discussed earlier is a case in point. Submission to the Torah is often the beginning of perpetual resistance and independence from alien ideologies. Just express the Torah view on any issue and see how many enemies you make. Tell a wealthy man that he is the custodian of God's wealth that has to be used in the manner prescribed by the Torah and he might consider you a radical socialist, a naive child or an educated lunatic. If the moral law of the Torah is the first and only force one must submit to, the burden of control is therefore lightened considerably as one fights for the rest of his life to preserve this integrity from the control of foreign influence. The Torah acknowledges that we are all slaves to God and the only choice is in the number of masters you want to have. "They are My servants" (Leviticus 25,55) and not the servants of servants.

CHAPTER V

A Short History of the Psychology of Religion

The application of 20th century psychological theories and instruments of measurement to the study of religion has produced a motley of small schools each of whose endeavours reflects a different error of approach. There is not much sustained interest in one approach to provide sufficient material to create a history. James' "Varieties of Religious Experience" (1901/1961) is a convenient starting point. He concluded that religious experience does indeed come in a variety of emotional forms, and that the origin of religious practices and personal peculiarities of the founders of religious sects cannot be used as measuring rods for religious utility. James was an independent thinker who often managed to reach his own conclusions contrary to the psychological climate of his day. However, in the area of religion he failed. When James was struck with the massive literature on religious experience that had been compiled for him, he could not free himself from the prevailing attitude of many university intellectuals who believed that one form of religious conviction was just as valid as another. He did not wish to investigate independently the diverse claims of religious schools in order to eventually extrapolate a set of criteria by which religions might be compared and evaluated. Instead he retreated historically into the early 19th century and allowed an idea of Jeremy Bentham to save him from the intellectual challenge. He concluded that from a utilitarian viewpoint, if the individual and society are benefitted from religious interest, that is sufficient self-justification for that sect.

The history of the successors to James is not a happy one. His student, Pratt (1920/1971), did not have the strength of character to resist the swell of religious criticism in the 20th century, and wrote an apology for his faith that has been followed by too many defensive coreligionists. All of these men made life unnecessarily difficult for themselves by assuming that the claims of whatever is current in the intellectual current of the times must be valid. They saw their problem as erecting a structure for the discipline of religion from whatever remained after the onslaught of the "scientists." James often ridiculed the trend to accept as valid whatever theories were constructed overnight from a few shreds of newly uncovered evidence. He was sophisticated about the conjectural gap between the narrow band of data and the megalithic theories built on them. He termed this ignorance "popular science." Pratt, however, simply accepted whatever attacks the Higher Bible Critics were making against the Hebrew Bible, as well as all the interpretative freedom Fraser gave himself in "The Golden Bough." In the end, by not adhering to his faith and adopting a more critical stance to every new folly, Pratt's mind was a collection of truisms which everyone considers false today.

James had another student, Starbuck (1911), whose mind more closely resembled his own. Against the friendliest advice of his colleagues who claimed that it couldn't be done, he set out to answer questions about religion by tabulating data that he had gathered from questionnaires. His graphs plot the data with clarity and the entire work is urbane and systematic. Starbuck was interested in the same phenomenon as James—that of conversion, or the sometimes gradual, sometimes sudden inner conviction of the truth and personal meaningfulness of religion. Starbuck records some interesting conclusions. Feelings of religious awakenings come most frequently at the age of puberty when growth in weight is most rapid. In spite of the general frankness of the responses to his questionnaire, in no instance was the sexual instinct said to be helpful to spiritual growth, nor was the religious life ever expressed in sexual terms. He concludes that, "The sexual life seems to have originally given the psychic impulse which called out the latent possibilities of development, rather than to have furnished the raw material out of which religion was constructed." (p. 402)

Starbuck also concluded that adolescence naturally divided itself into two periods. The first extends from 12 to 18 and the second from 18 to 25. The first is characterized by a burst of emotions that reaches its peak at about 15 or 16. The consciousness of self emerges at this time and a sense of personal responsibility for one's life. He says that these spontaneous feelings are often at odds with the fixed social system the adolescent finds himself in. Starbuck thus uses his data to confirm G. Stanley Hall's view of adolescence as a stage of storm and stress in the life of the individual. The period of 18 to 25 is one of rational adjustment to life through analyzing, building and following up bits of insight. Whereas James' book is really a selection of such conversion experiences as they were recorded in biographies and autobiographies, interspersing lengthy quotations with his own intelligent speculations, Starbuck provides some normative data. For the scholars of a few generations this topic of conversion formed the center of interest. Psychologists were not interested in the totality of religious experience, but only one small aspect which was prominent because of the strong evangelical activity of the time. The evangelists accepted certain experiences which they called religious, ran revival meetings and established educational institutions for the transmission of religious knowledge and dedication. The methods of psychology tested some of their common sense assumptions about the efficacy of their endeavors. The religious experience itself was not usually the subject of a psychological investigation, although James is a noteworthy exception. And he never got much beyond the descriptive stage. The data Starbuck accumulated when applied to the phenomenon answered many normative questions. His effort represents a certain use of psychology which is neglected in our own time.

With the current interest in moral development as it progresses under the direction of religious instruction, the utilization of psychological tests and simple descriptive statistics now seems a more fertile possibility than ever before. In fact, does the study of the Talmudic dialects not only sharpen the student's awareness of the existence of moral problems, but lead to the acquisition of decision making rules which he then applies to himself? What are those aspects of the educational procedure which lead to the internalization of moral values? Is one educational procedure more effective than another? A study of history suggests this to be the greatest service that psychology can perform for religion: as a practical test of theoretical hypotheses which originate in disciplines alien to psychology. The experience of religious quest, the deep calm consequent to spiritual discovery, and the feelings of sanctity following the performance of good deeds are all things for which there is no adequate vocabulary or measuring stick in the field of psychology. They can only be referred to metaphorically by describing something else.

The religious views of the psychologist Jung (Hostie, 1957) are hard to summarize because they were formulated in an obscure fashion. Jung also changed his mind on the subject over the years. Briefly stated, Jung believed that the unconscious mind of man has a grasp of the image of God. Man therefore first understands religion through his own personal experience, not as a teaching of a given religious group. The image or symbol of God that man recognizes is no fictitious creation of a disordered unconscious; quite the contrary, Jung insists that whatever exists in man's psychological experience exists in reality. No other path can reveal reality as well as that of the unconscious. One is religious to the extent that he allows himself to be affected by the powers that transcend consciousness.

The relevance of Jung's ideas to religion hinges on one major question—and that is the extent to which he claims that man's resourceful unconscious is able to grasp objective truth external to itself. There may be no richer source for our understanding of reality than the symbols of the unconscious, but do these symbols refer to what is true about the nature of God? At this point Jung appears to be a better psychologist than a theologian. After analyzing the dreams and verbal responses of his clients, Jung reaches some conclusions about human nature, not about metaphysics. In Jung's system our intuition of God would be valid if the nature of God and man were one. But if God is not only immanent in our lives but also absolute and transcendant, this aspect of His nature cannot be known experientially. It would not be reflected in the symbols of the unconscious and Jung's psychology cannot say anything about it.

The weakness in Jung's system is a direct result of the peculiarities of his own thought processes. In his autobiography (Memories, Dreams, Reflections, 1963), Jung records childhood experiences which have a hazy, intangible quality. He frankly admits that his mother was worried about him. This dreamy inability to separate the impressions of external sensation from the products of his own reveries is well reflected in the title of his autobiography. It reappears in his inability to decide whether God exists outside of our intuition of Him.

Freud's own personality likewise distinguishes his whole approach to religion. Far from the dreaminess of Jung, Freud was driving, ambitious, and anything but vague in his formulation. He was by education and inclination a thoroughly secular person. His theories are cold intellectual creations without any reference to religious experience. Nor did he ever seem to realize that statements of belief are derived from the manifold religious experience of mankind. He often voiced surprise that intelligent people were religious and by reversing the logic many a teacher, wishing to appear intelligent, has publicly disclaimed any allegiance to ritual religion.

Freud's central religious thesis (1932) was that our idea of God is psychologically a magnified father. He thought that a young person could easily lose his religious faith as soon as his father's authority ceased. The father figure was projected outward and identified as God. He felt that religion was another example of man's wishful thinking—a desire to escape from certain harsh aspects of reality into a world ruled by a benevolent force. The external world which one thought to be cruel and indifferent to human needs was transformed into a father-son relationship. He felt that if man would rely on his reason he would be able to outgrow the need for religion.

Freud hoped that psychology would eventually be able to explain away religion in the same way that a patient can be cured of a neurosis. This is very far from Jung who felt that religion is an essential activity of man. The unconscious contained an image of a father-like God which makes the child regard his human father as the image of God, not the other way around as Freud thought. As a symbol, the image of God is not a neurotic illusion but the most solid reality that can be known. To Jung, without the religious symbol man would first be ill.

It may surprise the reader, but the Talmud (Kidushin 30b) affirms Freud's speculation that a study of the image of the human father is a major method of arriving at an understanding of God. There are three partners in the creation of a person—his mother, his father and God. The respect due to one is the same as the respect due to another, and the punishment for cursing God is the same as for cursing one's parents. One sage, upon hearing his mother's footsteps would say, "I will rise before God who is coming." It is amazing that the Jewish mind in perpetual fear of idolatry and sensitive to alloying God's image with anything else, nonetheless never found anything potentially misleading about these parent-God comparisons. That God should be nothing but the product of these comparisons could only enter a mind frigid with indifference to the universal feelings of worshippers.

Jung seems to have left little mark on contemporary readers, and Freud's assumptions flourished for a few decades in the writing of the psychoanalytically oriented psychiatrists. We turn now to a consideration of the ideas of his followers.

The working assumptions of these writers are a few of Freud's dicta about the status of religion in the psychology of the individual as well as certain notions which he and early anthropologists assumed to be true. Among these are the belief that an inspection of primitive tribes today will reflect the origins of the religious systems of the West. If we see, for instance, a circumcision ceremony in some aboriginal people, then the meaning of the practice with all of its details must be applicable to the current Jewish practice of circumcision since it originally determined the act. Wherever the two differ, historical processes of change are called upon to account for the discrepancy, although it is considered as a mark of ingenuity on the researcher's part if he can take every current detail of practice in one group and find some parallel act in the other group, while making some allowances for a certain degree of distortion. A further assumption of the psychiatrists is that the unconscious is the repository of primitive ideas which reflect the distant past of mankind. Thus, if a client of theirs produces a dream in which religious objects occur, the association of these objects in the dream with incest, or other topics of sexuality and aggression, provides evidence for the origin of these objects in organized religion. Needless to say, by utilizing the ludicrous distortions of dreams as an explanatory device for grasping the basic truths of religion, the Freudians smuggly conclude with nothing but scorn and contempt for organized religion. As a pretext for understanding their client, they have devised a system by which he automatically is ranked inferior to them if he is religious because he has done less to refine the primitive aspect of his personality. He lives too close to his unconscious. As a group not physically aggressive, the psychiatrists encouraged compassion for such primitive types while at the same time deriding their ignorant attitudes.

Let us take Fromm-Reichmann's (1927) statements as

an example of the way the group works because her style is fairly typical. There is a Biblical injunction not to seethe a kid in its mother's milk, and this is taken as one of the sources for the Jewish prohibition against the simultaneous consumption of milk and meat. She says:

> Thus, by simultaneously consuming a male goat (= totem animal = father) and the milk of its mother, a man is committing the primal crime of incest. We may therefore assume that the ban upon the simultaneous consumption of flesh and milk is to be regarded in the first place quite generally as an unconscious defense against an incestuous wish. (p. 242)

She then turns to another injunction, that of not removing a mother bird from the nest at the same time as her young. She maintains, "Here again the removal of the creatures clearly signifies an identification with the mother bird and with her young, and their simultaneous removal signifies incest, which this prohibition therefore aims at preventing in the same way as does the prohibition of seething a kid in his mother's milk." (p. 242)

The difficulties that her explanation poses are numerous. If the removal of the two birds signifies an identification with them and their simultaneous removal signifies incest, and the very different behaviour of seething a kid in its mother's milk signifies the same thing, it is then impossible to specify any behaviours which won't signify incest. The meaning of every injunction of the Bible is then to prevent incest, as is every human action. If the goal of the prohibition is the prevention of incest, why would any law state the matter in such a round-about manner by couching the intention in the language of seething a kid in its mother's milk? And why repeat the matter in hidden form when as a matter of fact another

Biblical verse quite explicitly prohibits incest? Not letting the matter rest there, Fromm-Reichmann extends the meaning of the injunction:

> Seethe not the kid in his mother's milk, in the language of the unconscious, at the oral stage means: Thou shalt not seethe (cook) the son in the milk of his mother (= thy wife), i.e., thou shalt not cook, and therefore not eat, thy son.
> (p. 243)

In addition to the general prohibition against murder she thinks the Bible subtly forbids the killing and eating of children.

Now all of this "purely scientific and objective enquiry" sounds like the vindictive fury of a raving psychiatrist. It only becomes comprehensible when one analyzes the history of psychoanalysis to uncover a tactical error. Freud left a technology of therapy which could have been developed upon scientific grounds even though it might still remain more of an art than a science in the hands of the practicing therapist. His notion of transference, or the client's tendency to react to the counselor just as he did to some other significant person in his past, and the use of transference as a therapeutic variable of insight, was the beginning of a systematic approach to healing. It might have been analyzed into its parts, altered to suit the direction of new experimental evidence and developed as a means of understanding counselor and client interrelatedness. Instead, the psychiatrists early in their history made a tactical blunder by using the speculative and theoretical dicta of Freud's system to arrive at a correct "interpretation" of almost everything under the sun. They envied Freud's excursions into sociology, primitive societies, anthropology and literature, by which he bound the diverse areas into common unity with a few central themes of his theory, such as incest. They wanted to be like him, the self-appointed master of all human learning. Having little factual knowledge of these disciplines, they grasped at the latest speculative books and assumed what was transient and fragmentary to be permanently and comprehensively true. Some took the opinion of one sociologist, that Judaism is a basically matriarchal society, and then proceeded to apply psychoanalytic theory to Jewish practice. Others accepted the view of differing sociologists, that Judaism was basically a patriarchal religion, and applying the same principles to the same practices arrived at widely divergent conclusions.

The discipline of psychology differed from psychiatry by experimentally testing its propositions and changing its practices in accordance with the evidence. It understood that no single theory could possibly account for the complexities of life, and that all theories were therefore in trouble. As a result of continued experimentation, old ones were replaced with newer ones, and if the latter were not always superior to the former, a living discipline of intellectual enquiry was nonetheless established. Psychiatrists, on the other hand, did not want to hear that their theory was in error, and made an intellectual game of illustrating rather than testing the validity of their propositions. Their technology was one of ideas alone, and they became the least scientific of all the medical disciplines in the 20th century. Clinical psychologists now can claim that they are as prepared as anyone else to do therapy, and from personal observation those few who have a solid experimental background in learning theory are generally among the most competent.

CHAPTER VI

What Then is the Historical Achievement of Psychology?

As an obedient student of psychology I once calmly accepted the standard formulations which the textbooks used to describe the history of the discipline. They claimed that most schools of thought continued their altered existence in some new school of thought, a few theories died of neglect and almost none were experimentally proven to be wrong. My first reaction of skepticism to this philosophy of history which attributes the internal impetus for change to the logic of the ideas themselves was derived from an observation of the relationship between a theory and the personality that created it. The imposing influence of certain famous personalities whose books and articles are read with great interest seemed to indicate that the life work of leaders became the centre of focus around which all arguments rotated. From the time of its appearance in 1943, Clark Hull's *Principles of Behaviour* became the most important topic of interest in many university departments of psychology. In spite of the current attempt of neo-Hullians, and some of them clever psychologists at that, the whole system after Hull's death seems to be fading into obscurity. No one cares if the data contradicts Hull, and if the neo-Hullians can ingeniously show how their system can accommodate the data, the common reaction of others is "so what?" The longevity of the theory seems to be determined by the longevity of its author.

An examination of Wolpe's theory of systematic desensitization (Wolpe, 1958) in great detail tends to indicate that his single-minded and voluminous defense of his system helps to account for the current high interest in the theory. His reaction to experimentally based criticism is to ignore inflexibly the data by pointing out their shortcomings. This quibbling attitude allows him to return to the original formulation of 20 years ago. Ideally the establishment of a separate journal with himself as editor should have enabled him to elaborate on the initial claims with theoretical originality. Disappointingly, more case studies are accumulated and refinements are admitted in areas peripheral to major theoretical concern. There is no ongoing life work being constructed by Wolpe. His pretentious claims to have the most empirical of all systems of therapy has been gently derided in print.

Before any conclusions are drawn from this overview of current events, let us briefly review the theory. Wolpe began his work with the induction of experimental neuroses in cats. When he delivered an electric shock to the animals while they were confined in a small cage, Wolpe found that the anxiety response of the cats was conditioned to the cage and similar stimuli. Such anxiety was very resistant to extinction. Although they would not eat in their cages, the cats showed less anxiety in other rooms according to the lesser degree of resemblance which these bore to the original experimental room. The cats would feed with increasing readiness in rooms where their anxiety was not high enough to inhibit feeding. When he placed the cats in rooms that progressively approximated the original shock room, all signs of anxiety eventually disappeared.

At this time Wolpe discovered Jacobson's *Progressive Relaxation* (1938). This book showed him that relaxation could be used as a response to inhibit anxiety. Wolpe then formulated his principle of reciprocal inhibition: If a response incompatible with anxiety can be made to occur in the presence of anxiety-evoking stimuli, it will weaken the bond between the stimuli and the anxiety responses. Obviously, Wolpe assumed that human anxiety is similar to experimental anxiety insofar as both fall in the category of learned behavior which can be unlearned.

When reciprocal inhibition employs deep relaxation to inhibit anxiety, the treatment is called systematic desensitization. The procedure involves three sets of operations. First the client is trained in the technique of deep muscle relaxation. Next the client and the therapist construct a hierarchy of stimuli which provoke the anxiety response that is being treated. Finally, when the client is in a state of deep relaxation he is asked to imagine stimuli at the lower end of the hierarchy—those which arouse little anxiety. After the relaxation inhibits this small amount of anxiety, successively more provocative items of the hierarchy are imagined until the client is able to imagine the most feared situation with little or no arousal of anxiety. Automatic transfer to real life situations was reported by Wolpe.

Since the mechanical procedure of desensitization naturally falls into three separate units—the formation of the hierarchy, the induction of relaxation and the pairing of items from the hierarchy with relaxation, it was an open invitation to experimentalists to see whether any of

91

the elements could be altered without changing therapeutic results. If, for instance, the client could make just as much progress in fear reduction by sitting in a chair rather than progressively relaxing the muscle systems of his body, then a more convenient form of therapy would be demonstrated and Wolpe's theoretical rationale for the efficacy of the method would have to be revised. Others thought of contrasting the utility of the classical method with real life desensitization in which feared objects are not imagined but slowly approached so that the client's anxiety level is not raised too high. Carefully regulated successive approaches to the actual feared stimulus appear in some instances to be more potent anxiety reducers than imagined approach responses. These statements are some of the brief generalizations that ensue from reading through the mountains of material which have appeared in print since Wolpe's formulation first came to light.

What has happened to the original theory? A certain percentage of studies supports Wolpe while the rest is inconclusive or negative. And it must be acknowledged that some anxiety states or certain personality types are more amenable to one form of treatment than another. While all of this is true, it overlooks the fact that as a result of the research efforts aimed directly at investigating a given theory, that theory has been elaborated, refined and qualified far beyond the prophetic dreams of its author, and in spite of his resistance to the adaptation and reformulation of his original ideas. In attempting to show that the results are better explained by the laws of behavioural extinction than those of counterconditioning or reciprocal inhibition, other researchers have constructed new forms of experiments which have produced unexpected data requiring the formulation of new ideas to explain them. We are much more advanced in our understanding of psychology today than intellectuals who lived 500 years ago. If an idea about people was formulated at that time, the experimental tools were lacking to attack the central concept. Its own author was at a loss to elaborate on his notion, and many insights remained stored in aphorisms and pithy sayings for the lack of tools to handle the concepts. This explains the earlier reliance on authorities such as Aristotle or Ovid as a source of truth. It is not that earlier people believed in the intrinsic irrefutability of their favorite authors. This type of faith was reserved for the kind of knowledge which one could acquire only through revealed religion. They were not naive about Aristotle's fantastic speculations in biology; they simply had no way of knowing that he was wrong. The application of statistical techniques and research methodology to elementary psychological theories has enabled us to develop the tools of conceptual criticism that make us wise beyond the scope of our predecessors. An experiment begins as a test of some hypothesis but it eventuates in a richer conceptual language with which a student of psychology can criticize the hypothesis.

But even with this increased sophistication, in the current infancy of the discipline's history the use of psychological research as a truth criterion cannot be established. Wolpe will not conclusively be proven wrong. There is simply no decisive experiment the data of which can be used to refute or support his contentions that cannot bear an alternative interpretation. But the challenge to demonstrate him to be wrong has enriched the concepts we have about the acquisition and removal of fears and made it impossible for us to accept his simple statement on the basis of his authority. The technique of systematic desensitization is used with flexibility by many practicing therapists to great advantage. Now it is not one procedure, but a group of strategies in the armamentorium of the knowledgeable practitioner. The tools of psychological research are themselves the originators of new ideas on the old subject.

Unfortunately for the field, one cannot claim that a reverse relationship has been established. The acquired facility with conceptual criticism is not observed to be the source of new tools. Statistical mathematics is not indigenous to psychological theorization although one can ask a question that can only be resolved by the construction of a new statistic. The new statistic, however, cannot be derived from anything but a mathematical base. For example, it became apparent in the course of research on desensitization that the reported efficacy of the procedure might differ widely depending on the timing of the follow-up study. A six-month or a two-year interval led to divergent conclusions. The varied results of these follow-ups continue to surprise everyone with their unpredictability, though the methods used in the follow-ups were simply reapplications of those used at termination. A new idea was not a catalyst for the invention of a new tool.

From a historical perspective, Wolpe's system thrives on the conceptual productivity that lay hidden in a simple but ingenious three-step pairing of imagined fears with muscular relaxation. Without the mechanical invention of a concrete procedure, Wolpe could have written his quill to a stub and he might never have been read. It is easy to attribute Wolpe's discovery to the historical underpinnings which he himself uses as an explanatory hypothesis. Masserman worked with neurotic anxiety induced in cats, Sherrington spoke of the reciprocal inhibition of muscular systems, and Jacobson was relaxing his subjects. But a brief reading of other therapies current at the time leaves one with the impression that if he hadn't put all of these historical antecedents together in the special way he did, no one else would have. No other formulations were even remotely similar. There was no logic of invention which rested firmly on a supporting base. One doesn't read Masserman and Sherrington and feel himself forced to conclude as Wolpe did. The only recognizable similarity between Wolpe and his predecessors is the presence of some laboratory equipment. He was able to use old equipment in an original way because he was directed by hypotheses he had formulated in observing laboratory animals. These hypotheses were not logically related to anything historical; they were the creative product of a curious mind.

It is Wolpe's reliance on earlier theorists to explain his results which has in fact been repudiated most thoroughly. Hardly anyone accepts Wolpe's utilization of Sherrington's research as a valid explanation of the experimental results. The mechanical procedure of systematic desensitization was born of an interaction between an hypothesis and laboratory equipment. It stimulated research that has enriched our ability to analyze critically psychological concepts and has produced alternate mechanical systems as variants of the first. One may claim that all inventors are of necessity indebted to earlier workers, and this is certainly true of Wolpe. No one works in a historical and cultural vacuum. Because a new tool or the original use of an old one produces results which force new conceptualizations upon us, the history of psychology does not illustrate a logic of discovery by which one state of advancement necessarily forces the next stage into existence. It is the instruments of discovery and not past theories which produce data requiring the construction of new theories that is the primary directing force in psychological history. Why should these later conceptualizations be related logically to earlier ones?

Skinner's own historical account (Skinner, 1972) of his discoveries is another good example. Although he occasionally lapses into the typical pose of psychologists by pretending that some of his most important achievements happened somehow by chance, the document is nonetheless a record of the work of an inventive mind which constructed new boxes, alleyways, rope pullies, etc., to test hypotheses derived from his own observations of animals in the laboratory. The most rapid leaps in psychological discoveries occurred directly after the construction of the equipment. To be sure it takes a vigorous and inquisitive mind to pursue speculatively the interpretation of the data which the new apparatus produces. Like all agile thinkers he was quick to utilize anything surprising that chance or faulty equipment threw his way. At one point he borders on preaching to young psychology students about the way to discovery, as if you or I might close the book and then enter a laboratory where we could get on with the necessary work of creativity. Skinner's theory of operant conditioning is the product of mechanical inventions only related to existing laboratory experiments and preceding equipment in a most general way.

There is no question that theory and mechanical equipment interact in the progress of psychology. Skinner's series of inventions were separated by ideas, each invention the product of a new guiding hypothesis that preceded it. But this is not an example of the old problem of which came first, the chicken or the egg. It is in the area of technology that psychology is particularly deficient. The world has never been short of armchair speculation about the human condition. There just seems to be no easy way of establishing the validity of our theories of man. It is for this reason that the introduction of a new tool breaks the calm plateau on which earlier investigations rested and allows for the sudden spurt of discovery. When minds feel content on the new level of investigation, an orthodox school is founded around which the implications of the new data are elaborated. We now see this occurring in the field of operant conditioning.

Let us consider the degree of overlap between Skinner and his predecessors. By accepting physical determination in the psychological realm he obviously placed himself in the tradition of Watsonian behaviourism. And in his emphasis on the centrality of reinforcement to explain learning, Skinner at first glance seems to be pursuing Thorndike's "Law of Effect." Most historians of psychology have no theory of history beyond that of chronology and the overuse of the word "influence." Thus if both Thorndike and Skinner stress rewards and the former preceded the latter in time, we read that Thorndike influenced Skinner. In fact, physical determinism is a philosophical assumption elevated to scientific status by Enlightenment thinkers which attempts to answer the question, What is man?, and as such can never be substantiated by experimentation or unequivocally fixed by argument.

Skinner has shown that under a special set of circumstances the behaviour of pigeons in boxes is shown to some extent to follow certain regularities. And to a lesser extent reinforcement affects human behaviour. Skinner has successfully accounted for some of the regularities of observed behaviour and mistakenly labelled these as lawful. The number of variables that one must know to formulate a rough prediction of the running behaviour of a rat in a cage including the multitude of factors comprising the genetic limitations of the organism, the retained record of past learning and the current reinforcement contingencies of the environment, is of such magnitude, that to call this tottering superstructure of equations that constantly need the correction of each other a law (in the singular) of behaviour, grossly misrepresents the case. He cannot demonstrate a law of behaviour any more than Watson, because the concept itself is part of a philosophical given which one must accept before a certain type of laboratory experiment can be performed. No one can seriously confuse human determinism with his own understanding of daily human life without soon getting himself into considerable difficulty. One sees himself confronted constantly with alternatives which require a choice of action.

Skinner was not "influenced" by Watson's behaviourism. As soon as he entered an animal laboratory the technology made him a behaviourist. Skinner's personal acceptance of behaviourism as the key to the ultimately discoverable laws of all human behaviour is precisely the bold narrowmindedness which drew torrents of public criticism upon him from every intellectual circle. But this same narrowminded perception of just a few of the variables has led these intellectuals and a few psychologists to the cavalier rejection of all Skinner's work, and if the reader is saved by this essay from either of the polar extremities it has served its purpose.

If we examine the concept of reinforcement, it can be admitted that both Thorndike and Skinner use it in their theories of learning. But that is where the similarity ends. Thorndike defined it in terms of a satisfying or annoying state of affairs because he wanted to explain why it worked. Skinner gave a statistical definition of reinforcement by saying that it increased the probability of the response's occurrence, and thereby he sidestepped the entanglements of causal explanations. Thorndike applied reinforcement to explain the strength of a bond that was established between a stimulus and a response. Skinner's whole emphasis is on operant responses, those

The definition of psychology as an ongoing process of self-correction is such an idyllic view that one hesitates to disturb the tranquillity of those who choose to succumb to this gratifying thought.

As a brief example of the failure of psychology to correct its errors, one may cite the example of IQ screening. The era of IQ testing is now waning. For years it held sway with psychologists who were unaware that it correlated more with academic achievement than with any trait or substance which one could label as "intelligence." Teachers and the public became "great believers" in IQ as measured by the test, using it as a justification for the screening and special classification of students. It stood as a formidable barrier against progress in the study of child development because it led to constrictive thinking about a child's capacities, and it was unquestionably biased against minority groups. Unscrupulous bodies of legislators seeking to restrict immigration cited IQ to justify their racial criterion for the acceptance of white "Nordic" Europeans into a country, as opposed to "Mediterranean" and Slavic "elements" who had to be kept out. Kamin's (1974) book on the subject, *The Science and Politics of IQ,* is a quiet and factual indemnification of psychologists for their simplemindedness. The discipline will continue to lose its power of conviction with the educated masses as long as it continues to promise more than it can deliver, whether the product be psychotherapy, intelligence or moral reasoning.

Now that the errors of the IQ movement have been exposed, Kohlberg (1969) has constructed a written test which purports to measure stages of ability at moral reasoning. It has been long established that moral judgement, resistance to temptation when external constraints are absent, and feelings of guilt after transgression are not correlated with each other. Within each area, specific-

101

ity seems to be the rule. Aronfreed (1961), investigating responses to transgression, showed that there were no predictable relationships among specific types of reaction. One of the test's highest correlations was with IQ, for those who had greater verbal cunning produced written solutions to moral dilemmas which reflected higher stages of moral reasoning as outlined by the theory. One should really regard it as another test of IQ. The temptation to view a person as more moral because he is verbally brighter is too great for most people to resist, and the mind easily slips into this error even with forewarning. The test was once briefly introduced into a high school in the Province of Ontario for experimental purposes, with regrettable results. Teachers who discovered the low rank of some of their students then referred to them as "just a stage two-er." One who scores low in an intelligence test can still claim that if he is doing his best, what more can one reasonably expect from him? But low scores on a test of moral reasoning find no simple apology. One is responsible and answerable for his moral status. Someone cannot be punished for low ability at academic tasks, but punishments are constructed for the express purpose of rectifying those who can be more moral, but choose not to be. It is the area in which the law will not accept ignorance as an excuse.

Kohlberg's test is a potentially harmful innovation in education, and follows closely on our embarrassment over IQ. Moral status depends on the learning history of the child, his innate ego strength as it interacted with life experiences and the model of his parents, the nature and degree of temptation which providence has thrown his way, his momentary temperamental disposition as influenced by physiological fluctuation, and heaven knows what else. Where is the research that investigates the basic parameters of these variables and provides some normative data for a descriptive framework for moral development? The complexities of the moral development of man are so great that it was one of the few areas psychologists left for God, and Kohlberg, in tune with the recent public outcry over the lack of moral training for the young, has filled the vacuum with a lot of philosophical assumptions and a weak test. He then discovered that he and a few other chosen creatures had reached aesthetic levels of moral appreciation which could not be registered by the test, and consequently placed himself and Spinoza in a moral Nirvana. From this exalted position he looks down at kindliness, fair play and all the rest of human decency which makes life tolerable, labelling it "the bag of virtues." One is tempted to consider his endeavor ludicrous, if it weren't for its poor psychology and debased content.

As long as progress in psychology rests on technological and statistical advances that are derived from external disciplines, psychology cannot consider itself in charge of its own household. We all know that there is a momentous future in the development of cognitive behavior modification as an extension and modification of traditional behaviorism. The laurels now rest on the heads of men like Meichenbaum and Mahoney because of the way they have been able to operationalize concretely some procedures that altered cognitions. The area still awaits some more theoretical mind who will offer an expanded definition of cognition. Too many of the recent books on behavior modification lack of theoretical chapter altogether. This is a natural result of a discipline whose whole self-justification as a branch separate from philosophy derives not from its theoretical base but from some technology which is demonstrably useful. Such utility may have theoretical application in the laboratory or practical advantages in the office of a counselor. It will be easy to demonstrate that cognitive behavior modification works with a different technology from other forms of behavior modification, but it won't be so simple to show that its effects are superior. New forms will replace the old simply because they are chronologically later. The only enduring contribution of all these efforts is to be found in the advanced sophistication we now possess in handling concepts analytically, and through this function psychology has won its place in the intellectual history of mankind.

Since Koch (1976) has much to say about the history of psychology, a review of our similarities and differences is in order. He claims that most progress in psychology has been of a negative nature. After researching a given theory for a period of time researchers have learned that it was inadequate. A new theory is then invented and history sadly repeats itself. Although he admits that much positively useful data has accumulated through the researching of a given proposition, the overall and generalized impact is one of negation.

The experiments reviewed in this essay for a summary of systematic desensitization would indicate that we draw similar conclusions but evaluate them differently. No one can prove this or most other theories of psychology to be correct, and the absolute validity of the theory of desensitization is suspect given the wide range of alternate hypotheses that explain the data with equal facility. A psychological theory's greatest enemy is disinterest, not error. Once it is accepted that every psychological theory of man can never be more than a partial and incomplete perspective on only a single aspect of man's complexity which ignores more than it handles and is tied in a parochial way to the laboratory methodology from which it arose, then one can claim that the overall impact of desensitization is positive. Therapists have a convenient tool for anxiety reduction at their fingertips which appears reasonably effective. Our ability to analyze the parts of the desensitization procedure is highly enriched by our broader understanding of the role of mental imagery in the formation and maintenance of learned fears, and by the realization that for reasons yet to be verified the pairing of hierarchy items with responses other than relaxation (such as assertiveness) has its valid clinical application. One can agree with Koch that the theory is wrong if one sees it as an attempt to answer What is man? But as an explanation of one aspect of the multidimensionality of human experience, it has something to recommend it. This type of endeavor seems to be exactly what Koch has been calling for—limited in scope, and rigorous to the limits the concepts allow of methodological verification. In fact, if Koch's prescription for a future of psychologies in which different views of man's complexity are defined within the limits of each perspective, it would appear very much the way it looks now: fractionated, unreconcilable and irreducible.

Koch is led to more pessimistic conclusions than are necessary because his aim is prescriptive. If we would only discontinue our past modes of theorization, we would be ready for his perceptual definition of meaning and the forms of psychological investigation that would naturally ensue from it. But after studying his new psychological theory of meaning, it is hard to see how it would differ from the host of past theoretical attempts at internal revolutions or palace coups directed against most of the various forces holding prominence in the field. As a mere sketch of a proposal, it hardly has the persuasive power to stop thousands of experimenters in their footsteps at the sudden recognition of their conceptual error.

Koch's theory does have much to recommend it as another of the endless avenues investigating the many-sided views of man.

Koch has difficulty accepting the ultimate way in which psychology differs from other disciplines, although he accuses others of the same error. He is right that it cannot be a science like physics, nor is man something a computer model can fully describe. Psychologists are not merely in disagreement about the application of data in support of their theories; they cannot agree what an explanation of man would look like. The basic concepts of psychology will always be in dispute, for every theory requires a theory to justify its use as an account of man. Koch will not accept this ultimate difference between man and all other things that exist. So he constructs a theory which he claims will need no theory to justify it because it obviously fits man and not the artificial constructs of this pseudo-scientific discipline. But isn't that the whole question —what is man? If the nature of human nature is so obvious, why the history of discordant opinions? One would have to change man for Koch to be correct. He will just have to more deeply accept his own claim that psychology must be a set of different and differing disciplines. After reproving psychologists for their immodest claims, Koch proposes a theory which in order to be correct must make psychological history one foolish error. But what can be more immodest than the claim that only his theory fits man? What is man?

The major problem with systematic desensitization in the history of psychology is not the theory but the psychologists who investigate it. As soon as Lazarus (1971) grasped certain aspects of its utility, he went "beyond" it. His innovations appear less rigorously investigated than they naturally allow, and a record of the results on page 18 of his book testify to the failure of the innovations. Yet the book is read as a success story by the masses of psychologists who are eagerly running "beyond," supposedly to the hiding places of man's ultimate strength. The notion that mankind's worries are in part regulated by visual images of impending danger stored in the brain is of such worthy potential, that to grasp at something new is to make psychological history run ahead of itself. But more research has been done on the varied clinical application of desensitization than on the functioning of mental imagery. This headlong curiosity and approval of what is new to the neglect of what lies in hand is the source of the current crisis in psychology which Koch speaks about. It is not caused by a disillusionment with inadequate global theories of what is man, nor by a failure to reach some breakthrough in the central areas of learning and perception; it is the swelling of creative productivity by so many interested parties that cannot be held in focus long enough to formulate a school that deprives us of a sense of distinct past, present and future time. At first, psychological knowledge was lost in the explosion of experimental data, now to be followed by the rapid disappearance of psychological schools. Without the incisive criticism of a few leading personalities that rejects certain approaches and approves of others, there would be even less accomplished as the diversity of unevaluated psychological endeavor spreads beyond the comprehension of any one person.

I continue to marvel at the results of the few experiments on self-regulation reported in Thoreson and Mahoney (1974). Our ability to analyze what helps guide our behavior and the ensuing possibility of substituting unwanted for wanted control is of such luscious attractiveness, that for psychologists to abandon this frontier for the exaggerated promise of what lies beyond about which less is known, is to invite disorder as a privileged guest of the household.

It is worth the time to trace the history of technology in psychology to its origins. There is a stream of psychological thought (Joynson, 1970) which blames the slow progress of the discipline to its early acceptance of the model of physics. Just as mathematics are applied to certain experimental designs in physics, so should psychological research be constructed. There was a strong movement in the 1930's to introduce the concept of operationalism, then so popular in physics, as the guiding criterion for psychological validation. While the model of physical enquiry has had its effects on psychology, the philosophical underpinnings of modern psychological investigation are not derived from physics, but are to be found in the works of the 18th century Enlightenment thinkers.

Impressed with the success of the methodology of the natural sciences, the Enlightenment arbitrarily assumed that the same methodology could be applied to the social sciences as well. Just as scientific method had arrived at natural law such as the theories of Newton, so could it derive the proper rules for the regulation of society. The process of the application of scientific method to the conduct of man with the aim of discovering the rules of human behaviour was called "right reason." The phrase shows their belief that man was eminently a rational creature whose mind could vanquish superstition and ignorance when it was properly applied. It had failed in the past because the superstition of the church had overpowered reason. What society lacked in the past was harmony, but the establishment of peace and social justice as well as the elimination of crime were now feasible with their new found right reason. And reasonable people would naturally conform to the laws of human nature.

It is apparent that along with their faith in reason, was the belief in the perfectibility of man. Armed with the discoveries of right reason which provided the prescription for the correct environment, the moral and intellectual progress of mankind was inevitable. They grasped the utility of Locke's environmentalist view of the tabula rasa, man's mind as the clean slate on which anything could be written. Man's rationality would be insufficient for rapid progress if genetic traits imposed limitations on his alterability.

This overview of Enlightenment doctrine may be brief, but it is amazing how clearly modern psychology has never freed itself from the key 18th century concepts of the perfectibility of man and the validity of scientific research in the realm of social science. And this in spite of the obvious limitations of their philosophical speculations. Voltaire himself was a radical racist who felt that there were only four periods in the history of the world worth studying. All the rest was barbarism. Their goal to rid the world of "fanaticism" was pursued with a fanatical intensity that outstripped their victims. Their attacks on the church and its clergy were wild without measure. It was only Montesquieu who realized that society's values were relative. He saw that conditions of climate affect the laws that govern society and that what was good for one society was not good for another. It was this very attitude of tolerance which led him to be considered the black sheep among Enlightenment philosophers. Their worship of the goddess of reason was one of the most unreasonable acts of intellectual self-piety. Their rational contradictions do not end there, however. Along with their belief in the perfectibility of man was their acceptance of determinism in the physical as well as psychological realms. How progress is possible given man's inability to free himself from the potency of antecedent stimuli just strains one's reasoning power.

The Torah finds progress easy to explain because it postulates a spiritual force external to the world which lifts it up. The strivings of man for greater medical control of his body, the passion for more intense experiences of beauty, the search for knowledge that has no obvious practical benefit, and even the endless drive to accumulate more wealth than one requires, are understood by psychologists to be learned drives that impel man. The Torah views these activities as derivatives of an external force that pulls man upward: "And you should be as God" (Genesis 3,5). Stripped of its Biblical metaphors, this is the meaning of the Torah's concept of messianic redemption. God pulls on man, and man responds with striving.

The work of modern psychologists as students of the Enlightenment allows us to place the cult of personality in sharper perspective. If most of the fundamental issues are incorporated in the philosophy of a given school and are simply accepted by its adherents as working hypotheses, then all innovations are merely superficial in character. Skinner has not replaced Thorndike on any question because neither constructed a theory or discovered a technology which enabled psychology to alter the metaphysical views of the Enlightenment philosophers. The achievement of individual psychologists elaborate on certain aspects of human behavior and thereby give their claims a more substantive scientific basis. Personality functions to keep alive the hope that the discipline will some day be able to introduce the criterion of truth into metaphysical attempts to answer What is man?

No doubt all of these theoretical limitations are of little concern to the modern psychologist as long as the technology of his research produces results of some utility. And with nothing but religious philosophy offering an alternative to the 18th century claim that scientific methodology ensures the advancement of social science, they will no doubt continue on their present course. Given the prestige of science, there is little chance that psychologists will relinquish their faith for discovering Newtonian order in the world of man.

CHAPTER VII

Psychology in the Book of Job

This book concludes with a study of the Book of Job because it is an example of one way in which the Torah has answered the question, What is man? By analyzing the dialogue between Job and his comforters it is also possible to learn something about the counselor-client relationship.

The wonderful book of Job entices the readers by presenting dramatically some of the perplexing problems of all thinking people in the most beautiful form of narrative and poetry. But as one draws close to it, the special way the question of why good people suffer is opened, and more importantly, the resolution of these difficulties begins to recede and become dim, leaving the reader with the resounding impression of grandeur and magnificence. The remaining intellectual task of providing an answer from the raw material of the story is so formidable, that perhaps no other book of the Bible has been surrounded with so much unsettled and contradictory opinion. Some Sages claim that Job was a historical figure,

113

while others claim that he was invented to point a moral. The time of the story has been relegated to the era of Moses or Ezra, quite a few centuries apart. And Talmudic opinion is divided as to his Jewish or Gentile identity. Therefore the ensuing comments can only be consistent with some but not all interpretative approaches.

In chapter one, Job is presented as a upright man who enjoys life in the fullest sense. Of course, being slightly old fashioned, he still considers children as a source of unmitigated happiness. He delights in the family solidarity shown by his children who go to considerable expense and trouble to organize a constant round of lavish meals which promote family togetherness. His individual personality is clearly described from the start (1,5). In spite of the fullness of his blessings, Job is a man perpetually gripped by fear of wrongdoing and some consequent impending punishment. In the hope of avoiding calamity, he rises early to make atonement for his children who may have sinned in their hearts. And then the very thing which he fears suddenly happens. All the joy of his children and himself that he tried to preserve undisturbed is reft from his hands through one disaster following close upon another. "For the thing which I did fear is come upon me" (3,25). The book reiterates that with all this Job did not sin with his lips. One Talmudic opinion maintains that with his lips he did not sin, though he did harbour sinful thoughts in his heart. Curiously, Job persistently questioned his children's integrity. Their behaviours and speech seemed correct, but who knows what intentions a man's mind produces that remain hidden from everyone but God! Using the mechanism of projection, he was suspicious of his children for that weakness which he vaguely recognized in himself. In an attempt to purge one's guilt for some shortcoming, a person offers some of the heftiest criticism to others for their supposed possession of that very defect.

What were the sufferings of Job? He lost his wealth, his children, and was then afflicted with boils from his head to his feet (2,7). As he sat among the ashes, his wife advised him to find some method of destroying himself. All of Job's pains seemed tolerable, until he was maimed physically in such a way that he was brought to public disgrace. Even his own friends were unable to recognize him (2,12). "And he took a potsherd to scrape himself with; and he sat among the ashes" (2,8). The self-disgust generated by scratching his boils while surrounded by filth was accentuated when others began to view him in the same light. Surely, the likeness of God had departed from him and he had become a caricature. At this point his wife said that man can endure all suffering except for degradation in the sight of others. Death is a preferable state to loss of social standing. This aspect of his suffering is brought to light by the observations of a woman, and we are indebted to the book for this fine insight into feminine psychology. Job's male friends are impressed with the physical dimensions of his suffering, but a woman's heightened social sensitivities enables her to realize that his altered physical appearance can cause a far more painful social anguish. This Biblical insight into the depths of human behaviour has been confirmed by modern psychology which now recognizes social class differences as a major variable affecting experimenting results. All of us can agree that so much of our behaviour operates within the restraints of what we consider socially acceptable, and many of our decisions are based on "who we think we are."

In the midst of his public disgrace, Job's three friends arrive simultaneously to comfort him, but in actuality they form a small court that will sit in judgement upon him. Each one in turn states his own opinion, and repeats some of the views of his friends as well, in a cyclical fashion of dialogue with Job. This procedure creates some confusion if one anticipates three separate lines of thought. It is possible that the author of the book (which one Talmudic opinion ascribes to Moses) did this in order to make three opinions look like one. After all, the friends are unanimous in their conclusion that Job must have sinned against God and has deserved his misfortunes. All three are rejected emphatically by Job who will not accept that his personal failings are the cause of misfortune. They are wrong in saying he suffers because he sinned, and he will not relinquish his standpoint until God grants him a personal audience in which he may justify himself and request an explanation from God.

In their judgemental stance towards Job, his friends are not like modern counselors. They seem more determined to offer intellectual explanations and advice than in commiserating with Job's wounds. And Job repeats his warning that they will be punished for saying he has sinned. In other ways they are ideal friends. They travel great distances to comfort him, and their physical presence in the time of his distress is itself a great consolation. The friends look at his reduced figure and gauging the severity of his condition, refrain from speaking until Job opens with a description of his suffering (2,13). It is only possible to counsel someone when the subjective framework within which he experiences his life is expressed. The value, mores and personal views of the client are the limitations within which counselors are forced to work. Since their view of Job's guilt is outside of his own frame of reference, they are easily led to the edge of verbal cruelty. Unable to align themselves with his own view of his life, they leave little permanent impact upon him.

116

We know from the beginning and end of the book that Job enjoyed great prosperity both before and after his suffering. It is proper then to inquire what length of time the middle of the book occupies, that period of dialogue with his friends which is roughly equal to the length of his suffering. Some opinions say he was afflicted for a year, others say two. When considering the entire Book of Job, one Rabbinical opinion claims that this is an example of a man who consumed so much of the merits for his righteousness through pleasure in this world, that no afterlife was possible for him. This is a classical example of the startling insights of our Sages. The whole world sees Job's plight as that of a good man suffering the utmost forms of physical distress and psychological grief. They have coined the phrase "the sufferings of Job." And then we are told that here we have an example of someone who enjoyed life to satiety and received no reward in the hereafter! This position is arrived at by carrying certain facts to their logical conclusion. If he only suffered for a year or two, and this was both preceded and followed by many years of health, wealth, and the joys of a close knit family, then the Book of Job must illustrate how good people prosper! If there is a question at all about divine providence in the case of the righteous, it only arises through a magnified view of a small segment of life which cannot be wholly grasped.

The bulk of the book is devoted to Job's questioning of God's management of the world, and for quantity alone it leads the reader to question the foundation of his faith just as Job does. At points Job comes close to accusing God of error. The initial and final chapters of the book which briefly describe Job's lifelong felicity leave little emotional impact on the reader who is taken aback by the horror of Job's suffering. In spite of the fact that the Rabbis noted the disproportional representation of plea-

117

sure and pain in the chapters of the book, nowhere do we find any historical record of their attempt to conceal this complex work from public view. The Book of Ezekiel was thought to contain verses which contradicted the Torah, and for this reason there was a movement to prevent it from misleading people who would scan through the pages superficially. When a sufficiently lucid explanation of its difficulties was finally composed, the Book of Ezekiel was then taught universally without restraint. Credit must be given to the openmindedness of Rabbinical thinking which allowed a work with a seemingly misleading emphasis like Job to be studied publicly without question.

In Chapter 32 the young figure of Elihu is introduced. Although he rejects the words of the older comforters, out of respect for age he waits for them to conclude before he expresses his views. In Chapter 38 God finally appears and addresses Job out of the whirlwind. Strangely enough, the structure of the book leads us to believe that earlier difficulties will be resolved; in these final chapters, however, the content of Elihu's words at first glance seems to repeat the opinions of the three friends whom he has just scorned. And the difficulty in understanding God's answer has given rise to considerable interpretative disagreement. Working with hints from Maimonides, the following ideas rest most easily with me. Job is taught something at the end of the book which makes the whole difference in his life. For all of the phrases of righteousness by which Job is described, he is never lauded for great wisdom. His piety is simple, because he has gained his understanding of God through tradition not via an ongoing search like Abraham who was also put to the test. Through his sufferings and the final message of the book he learns of God through experience. As a man blessed with material wealth and familial bliss, Job is unaware of the pleasures associated with the study of Torah which leads to a deepening awareness of God. Elihu gives him his first lesson in Torah. If an afflicted person has one intercessor who pleads on his behalf the decree against him is sometimes lifted and he is returned to good health. But intercession and deliverance do not always automatically follow each other. There are too many considerations in this complex world.

God's message to Job then amplifies on Elihu's answer by explaining one of the major complexities that often make human suffering incomprehensible. The point is made metaphorically through examples drawn from the natural world. The huge fish leviathan is described by God as covered with scales that are pressed so closely together that no air can come between them (41,7). Joined together in an exact formation they cannot be parted (41,9). God asks Job who gave the horse his strength to leap (39,19-20) and the hawk the wisdom to fly south (39,26). All of the miraculous phenomena of nature are expressed in terms of the great and wondrous difficulty of their creation. Equally significant are the innumerable laws of nature whereby God in a sense restricts his own creativity. The instinctive habits of the horse and the hawk cannot be altered once God has set them. From the outset, the text utilizes an anthropomorphic description of God deliberately and consciously limiting his own omnipotence to work within the limits of creation. Job's sufferings arise because of an agreement that God makes with Satan. It has nothing to do with Job's worthiness, although Job does not become aware of this immediately.

Unless the book is interpreted in such a way that God's ways are made known to man, a very considerable problem will remain unsolved. Why does not God tell Job finally why he suffers? What is the meaning of God's appearance at the end of the book if it doesn't answer Job's

119

question? By increasing example upon example, Job learns the lesson that the reader knew at the beginning. Satan has been given certain powers by God, and he exercises them in forcing God's hand, so to speak, into an arrangement by which a test of Job is devised. In order to express this idea so that human ears can understand it, God addresses the heavenly court praising Job before the accusor. This gives Satan an opening to demand of God the right to put Job through a series of trials. According to God's self-limiting rules, he cannot deny him this request. But Satan is restricted as well. God allows him to afflict Job but prohibits the taking of his soul. One Rabbinic opinion maintains that Satan's sufferings were worse than Job's. It is like telling a man to break a jar and at the same time warning him not to spill the wine. The jar is a symbol of the body of Job, and the wine a symbol of his soul. Satan's conformity to God's instructions is reflected in the ailment of boils which cause great pain by attacking the external parts, while the internal vital organs that protect life are left untouched.

The overall message of the book's conclusion is arrived at through a metaphorical presentation of God's heavenly household, the forces of creation which are separate from the world of man. Job errs in thinking that every human experience on earth has an explicable counterpart in heaven. God often occupies himself with other forces of creation which are dissociated from man, although they may affect him grievously. The key concept in grasping God's preoccupation with his heavenly court is that once relationships are established and rules of conduct are formulated, freedom is automatically narrowed. The infinite complexity of the natural world alone, that of the horse, fish and bird, excluding the greater intricacy of man, is of monumental and staggering proportions; yet once God created this incredibly complex universe he built in laws of nature, or certain regularities, and consciously limited his freedom to tamper with it. This in essence is God's message to Job when He asks him to regard the scales of the fish.

When Job grasps this aspect of God's revelation, his perspective of the problem is greatly altered. "I had heard of you by the hearing of the ear, but now my eye sees you. Therefore I abhor my words, and repent, seeing I am dust and ashes" (42,5-6), Too often the commentators (Gordis, 1965) are overwhelmed by the power of the poetic description of the huge force behind the elements of nature. They mistakenly conclude that it was God's intention to demolish Job and his problem as insignificant by comparison. But where do we find Jewish prophecy that aims to destroy man's integrity? Didn't Abraham and Moses receive answers to their questions of God's rule? Is it a Jewish ideal not to question? Job would not rest until God directly answered him. To imagine that God wanted to obliterate Job is not a Jewish pattern of thought. The very last lines of Job are an expression often found on the lips of Torah scholars whose research into life lead them from one level of understanding to the next. They are in a state of perpetual repentance over their earlier more limited perspective. Job learns that the knowledge of God is one of man's greatest joys and achievements.

We assume that as soon as God directly addressed Job his physical sufferings were at an end. But he was still not restored to his earlier delights of prosperity. However, God does express his anger at Job's friends for their lack of sympathy and their hasty condemnation of their friend. Now seeing that his friends had incurred God's wrath (42,7) and stood in jeopardy for not having said the right thing to Job, Job senses the reversal in their positions. He does not lose a moment in availing himself of the opportunity to help them. He prays for them, and has his own cause answered first. "And the Lord changed the fortune of Job, when he prayed for his friends" (42,10). The knowledge that Job attained as a result of his own revelation was insufficient reason for God to restore his earlier status. It was only when the new wisdom was translated into concrete behaviour that there was any evidence that he truly understood it. The act of prayer shows that as a result of his faith which finally surmounted the barrier of silence, Job reestablished a deeper relationship with God. But this relationship proceeded by steps: the end of suffering and the restitution of what was lost. This affirms the Jewish position that for completion man needs the physical comforts of family and wealth as well as the spiritual knowledge of God, and refutes the opinions of those who claim that the final chapter of God's blessings was simply added to the text as a sop to console the frightened reader.

REFERENCES

All references with an a or b after the page number, such as Kidushin 13a, are citations from the tractates of the Babylonian Talmud, available in English translation from the Soncino Press, London.

Allinsmith, W. The learning of moral standards. In D. R. Miller & G. E. Swanson (Eds.), *Inner conflict and defense.* New York: Holt, 1960, pp. 141-176.

Amsel, A. *Judaism and Psychology.* New York: Feldheim, 1969.

Amsel, A. *Rational-irrational man.* New York: Feldheim, 1976.

Aronfreed, J. The nature, variety and social patterning of moral responses to transgression. *Journal of Abnormal and Social Psychology,* 1961, *63,* 223-240.

Ausubel, D. P., & Sullivan, E. V. *Theory and problems of child development* (2nd ed.). New York: Grune & Stratton, 1970.

Boring, E. G. *Sensation and perception in the history of psychology.* New York: Irvington, 1942.

Bulka, R. P. Setting the tone: The psychology-Judaism dialogue. *Journal of Psychology and Judaism,* 1976, *1*(1), 3-13.

Burwen, L. S., & Campbell, D. T. The generality of attitudes toward authority and nonauthority figures. *Journal of Abnormal and Social Psychology,* 1957, *54,* 24-31.

Davison, G. C., and Stuart, R. B. Behavior therapy and civil liberties. In C. M. Franks and G. T. Wilson (Eds.), *Annual review of behavior therapy,* Vol. 4. New York: Brunner/Mazel, 1976.

Ethics of the Fathers. New York: Feldheim.

Eysenck, H. J. The effects of psychotherapy: An evaluation. *Journal of Consulting Psychology,* 1952, *16,* 319-324.

Freud, S. *Leonardo da Vinci.* London: Kegan Paul, 1932.

Freud, S. *Moses and monotheism.* New York: Random, 1939/1955.

Freud, S. The psychogenesis of a case of homosexuality in a woman (1920) vol. 18. *The complete psychological works of Sigmund Freud.* London: Hogarth, 1955.

Fromm-Reichmann, F. Das jüdische speiseritual. *Imago,* 1927, *13,* 235.

Gordis, R. *Book of God and man: A study of Job.* Chicago: University of Chicago Press, 1965.

Hartshorne, H., & May, M. A. Studies in the nature of character (Vol. 1). *Studies in deceit.* New York: Macmillan, 1928.

Heider, F. *The psychology of interpersonal relations.* New York: Wiley, 1958.

Holroyd, J. C., & Brodsky, A. M. Psychologists' attitudes and practices regarding erotic and nonerotic physical contact with patients. *American Psychologist,* 1977, *32*(10), 843-849.

Hostie, R. *Religion and psychology of Jung.* London: Sheed & Ward, 1957.

Hull, C. *Principles of behavior.* New York: Appleton, 1943.

Hull, C. *A behavior system.* New Haven: Yale University Press, 1952.

Jacobson, E. *Progressive relaxation* (2nd ed.). Chicago: University of Chicago Press, 1938.

James, W. *Varieties of religious experience.* New York: Macmillan, 1961.

Joynson, R. B. The breakdown of modern psychology. *Bulletin of the British Psychological Society,* 1970, *23,* 261-269.

Jung, C. G. *Memories, dreams, reflections.* New York: Pantheon, 1963.

Kamin, L. *The science and politics of IQ.* Potomac, Md.: Erlbaum, 1974.

Klahr, C. N. Science versus scientism. In A. Carmell & C. Domb (Eds.), *Challenge.* Jerusalem: Feldheim, 1976.

Koch, S. Language communities, search cells, and the psychological studies. In *Nebraska symposium on motivation, 1975.* Lincoln: University of Nebraska Press, 1976, pp. 477-559.

Kohlberg, L. Stage and sequence: the cognitive-developmental approach to socialization. In D. A. Goslin (Ed.), *Handbook of socialization theory and research.* Chicago: Rand, McNally, 1969.

Kuhn, T. S. *Structure of scientific revolutions.* Chicago: University of Chicago Press, 1970.

Lasker, A. A. Motivation for attending high holiday services. *Journal for the Scientific Study of Religion.* 1971, *10,* 241-248.

Lazarus, A. A. *Behavior therapy and beyond.* New York: McGraw-Hill, 1971.

Maslow, A. *Motivation and personality.* New York: Harper, 1954.

Maslow, A. *Religions, values, and peak-experiences.* New York: Viking, 1971.

Matarazzo, R. G. Research on the teaching and learning of psychotherapeutic skills. In A. Bergin & S. Garfield (Eds.), *Handbook of psychotherapy and behavior change.* New York: Wiley, 1971, pp. 895-924.

Mednick, M. T., & Mednick, S. A. *Research in personality.* New York: Holt, Rinehart & Winston, 1963.

Mischel, W. *Personality and assessment.* New York: Wiley, 1968.

Paquda, Ibn. *Duties of the heart.* New York: Feldheim.

Pratt, J. B. *The religious consciousness: A psychological study.* New York: Hafner, 1971.

Rabinovitch, N. L. *Probability and statistical inference in ancient and medieval Jewish literature.* Toronto: University of Toronto Press, 1972.

Rensberger, B. Briton's classic IQ data now viewed as fraudulent. *New York Times,* November 28, 1976.

Rogers, C. R. The necessary and sufficient conditions of therapeutic personality change. *Journal of Consulting Psychology,* 1957, *21,* 95-103.

Rogers, C. The concept of a fully functioning person. *Psychotherapy,* 1963, *1,* 17-26.

Serber, M., Hiller, C., Keith, C., & Taylor, J. Behavior modification in maximum security settings: One hospital's experience. *American Criminal Law Review,* 1975, *13,* 85-99.

Skinner, B. F. Cumulative record: *A selection of papers* (3rd ed.). New York: Appleton, 1972.

Spero, M. H. On the relationship between psychology and Judaism. *Journal of Psychology and Judaism,* 1976a, *1*(1), 15-33.

Spero, M. H. The critical review. *Journal of Psychology and Judaism,* 1976b, *1*(1), 83-84.

Spero, M. H. The critical review. *Journal of Psychology and Judaism,* 1977, *2*(1), 89.

Starbuck, E. D. *The psychology of religion.* New York: Scott, 1911.

Thoreson, C. E., & Mahoney, M. J. *Behavioral self-control.* New York: Holt, Rinehart & Winston, 1974.

Truax, C. B., & Carkhuff, R. R. For better or for worse. In *Recent advances in the study of behavior changes.* Montreal: McGill University Department of Psychology, June, 1963.

Truax, C. B. and Carkhuff, R. R. *Toward effective psychotherapy: training and practice.* Chicago: Aldine, 1967.

Watson, J. B. *Behaviorism.* New York: Norton, 1925.

Wikler, M. The Torah views of mental illness: Sin or sickness? *The Yeshiva Educator's Notebook,* January, 1978, pp. 1-4.

Williams, R. M. *American society.* New York: Knopf, 1960.

Wolpe, J. *Psychotherapy by reciprocal inhibition.* Stanford: Stanford University Press, 1958.

Wolpe, J. *The practice of behavior therapy* (2nd ed.). New York: Pergamon, 1973.

INDEX OF NAMES

Maslow, A., 21, 24, 28, 42
Masserman, J., 94, 95
Matarazzo, R. G., 33
May, M. A., 43, 44
Mednick, M. T., 13
Meichenbaum, D., 103
Mischel, W., 42
Montesquieu, Baron de, 109
Moses, 10, 114, 116, 121
Newton, I., 19, 108, 111
Ovid, 93
Pavlov, I., 13
Piaget, J., 59
Pratt, J. B., 78
Rabinovitch, N. L., 54
Rambam (see Maimonides), 64
Rav, 56
Rav Chanina, 32
Rav Huna, 46
Rensberger, R., 5
Rogers, C., 11, 12, 28
Rousseau, J., 28
Satan, 119, 120
Saul, King, 38

Sennacherib, 49
Serber, M., 14
Shakespeare, W., 49
Sherrington, C., 94, 95
Shmaya, 49
Skinner, B. F., 65, 69, 70, 72, 73, 96, 97, 98, 99, 110
Solomon, King, 64
Spero, M., 21, 22, 23
Spinoza, B., 103
Starbuck, E. D., 79, 80
Stuart, R. B., 14
Sullivan, E., 42, 44
Thoreson, C. E., 107
Thorndike, E., 97, 98, 110
Truax, C. B., 12, 15
Voltaire, 109
Watson, J., 13, 97, 98
Wikler, M., 38
Williams, R. M., 74
Wolpe, J., 13, 90, 91, 92, 93, 94, 95, 99, 100
Wundt, W., 4
Yochanan, 49, 73
Zechuriah, 33